COMMANDER'S PALACE

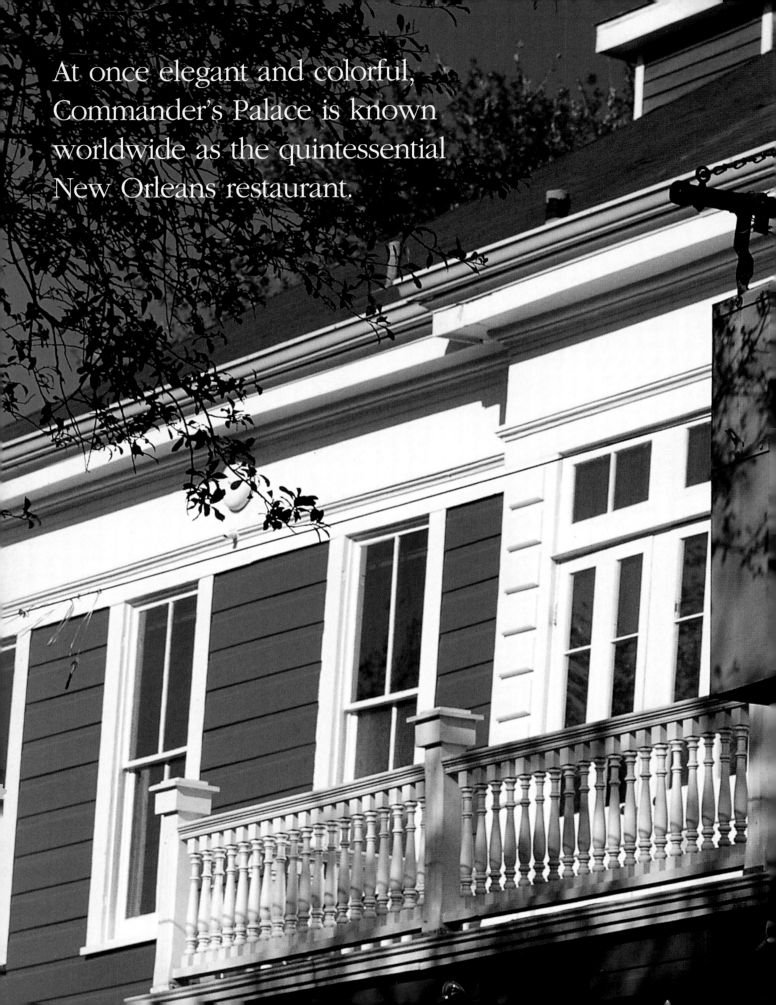

At once elegant and colorful, Commander's Palace is known worldwide as the quintessential New Orleans restaurant.

Also in the Great Restaurants of the World series:

Café des Artistes
Charlie Trotter's
The Inn at Little Washington
The Sardine Factory

COMMANDER'S PALACE

An Insider's Look at the Famed Restaurant and Its Cuisine

Rayna Skolnik

Photographs by Lee Celano and Kurt Coste

Lebhar-Friedman Books

New York • Chicago • Los Angeles • London • Paris • Tokyo

Lebhar-Friedman Books
425 Park Avenue
New York, NY 10022

Published by Lebhar-Friedman Books
Lebhar-Friedman Books is a company of Lebhar-Friedman, Inc.

Great Restaurants of the World® is a trademark
of Lebhar-Friedman Books.

Printed in the United States of America

Library of Congress Cataloging-in-Publication Data

Skolnik, Rayna
      Commander's Palace : an insider's look at the famed
restaurant and its cuisine / Rayna Skolnik.
          p. cm. — (Great restaurants of the world)
      ISBN 0-86730-802-8 (alk. paper)
      1. Commander's Palace (Restaurant) 2. Cookery,
American—Louisiana style. I. Commander's Palace (Restaurant)
II. Title. III. Series.

      TX945.5.C62 S56 2000
      641.5'09763'35—dc21
                                        99-059966

Book design: Nancy Koch, NK Design

An SCI production

Jacket design: Kevin Hanek
Photographs © 2000 by Lee Celano and Kurt Coste

Visit our Web site at lfbooks.com

Volume Discounts
This book makes a great gift and incentive. Call
212-756-5240 for information on volume discounts.

Dedication

To my husband, Marty, my partner in all of life's adventures, culinary and otherwise

Rayna Skolnik's interest in international cuisines led her to study with Julie Sahni, and she helped prepare the manuscript for Sahni's first book, *Classic Indian Cooking.* Skolnik also studied with Henry Hugh, owner-chef of a restaurant in New York City's Chinatown, and she has written for the "Mail Order Gourmet" newsletter and for "Chefs' Secrets," a newsletter published by the Food Network. She has traveled on assignment to China, Austria, France, Russia, Israel, England, Holland,

Germany, Scandinavia, Greece, Turkey, and Australia, happily tasting all the way.

Skolnik is the author of *Effective Delegation: The Key to Successful Management; Mastering the Business Interview; The Retirement Planning Guide;* and the *Trade Show Exhibitors Association Guide to Successful International Exhibiting.* She and her husband live in New York City's Greenwich Village within walking distance of such culinary resources as Chinatown, Little Italy, Little India, and the Union Square Greenmarket.

Lee Celano, a photojournalist who covered such hot spots as El Salvador, Somalia, and Haiti, moved to New Orleans in 1996 and quickly discovered that the focus of life in the Crescent City is the dinner table. He spent three years there, capturing the essence of Louisiana cooking on film for such magazines as *Wine Spectator* and *Food and Wine* and doing portraits of some of the city's best chefs. Other projects included photo essays on jazz funerals, Mardi Gras Indians, community policing in New Orleans housing projects, and modern-day Cajuns of Southwest Louisiana. In 1999, Celano returned to his hometown of Los Angeles, where he works for such national publications as *The New York Times, Chicago Tribune, Newsweek, Sports Illustrated,* and *People.*

Kurt Coste, who has been a commercial photographer in New Orleans since 1980, has seen his work published in more than 40 nations. He has won numerous awards for excellence in fashion photography and advertising and in 1985 was named the American Advertising Federation's Photographer of the Year for New Orleans. Coste's clients include the Louisiana Superdome and Sports Arena, BellSouth, the French Market Association, Carl Zeiss North America, Volunteers of America, Atlas Van Lines, Hitachi Telecom USA, and the New Orleans Symphony and Ballet.

CONTENTS

FOREWORD

Few experiences in life enhance the joy of living more than a fine dining experience. The ambience, style, service, food, and presentation of a great restaurant are all elements that add immensely to enjoying a culinary adventure. Many restaurants provide customers with a consistent dining experience, and a number of these are truly outstanding. Only a few, however, exceed the expectations of even their most discerning patrons. They deserve to be called great, and we are proud to recognize them

as Great Restaurants of the World. The first five restaurants in this series of books are:

Commander's Palace
Café des Artistes
Charlie Trotter's
The Inn at Little Washington
The Sardine Factory

These beautiful books have been a labor of love and dedication for all the parties involved. We have called upon the editors of *Nation's Restaurant News,* the leading business publication serving the restaurant industry, to assist us in developing the criteria for the Great Restaurants of the World series and in choosing the candidates. We think you will agree that the selections are of great interest and merit.

All of the Great Restaurants of the World represent a unique creative spirit of providing the public with a meaningful dining experience. However, they also share many of the same traits. Most significantly, each was founded by one or more persons with the kind of entrepreneurial energy dedicated to achieving excellence. Without exception, these founders instilled in their organizations a single compelling mission: to provide their guests with the ultimate dining experience. Food and food presentation are always the first priority. After that come service, ambience, and value.

All of these restaurants have been successful by paying attention to innumerable small details every day, every week, and every month throughout the year. Each has proved many times over its reputation as a truly great restaurant through the loyalty of its repeat customers and the steady stream of awards and recognition it has received over the years, both from its guests and from its peers.

This book and the others in the series are your invitation to experience the Great Restaurants of the World, their history and their heritage. Savor every page and enjoy the adventure.

James C. Doherty
Executive Vice President
Lebhar-Friedman, Inc.

Awards

Some of the awards presented to Commander's Palace

AAA Four Diamond 1999

Mobil Four Star 1999

James Beard Foundation
Outstanding Service in the United States 1993
Outstanding Restaurant in the United States 1996
Best Chef in the Southeast 1999

Chefs in America
New Orleans Chef of the Year 1992

Condé Nast Traveler
Top Restaurant in New Orleans and Vicinity 1995

Distinguished Restaurants of North America (DiRōNA)
Award of Excellence 1993-2000

Food and Wine **magazine**
No. 1 Restaurant in the United States 1995
Quintessential New Orleans Restaurant 1998
Best Value in New Orleans 1998

Nation's Restaurant News
Fine Dining Hall of Fame 1982

New Orleans **magazine**
Chef of the Year 1996
Readers' Choice Top Chef 1998

The Robb Report for the Luxury Lifestyle
Best of the Best—No. 2 Chef in the World 1999

Sales & Marketing Management
Business Executives' Dining Awards
No. 1 in the United States 1986

Southern Living
No. 1 City Restaurant 1996
Reader's Choice Award 1997-1999

Travel & Leisure
Critic's Choice Award 1996

Wine Spectator
Critics' Choice in New Orleans 1995
Award of Excellence for Wine 1998

Zagat Survey
Most popular restaurant in New Orleans 1996-1999

Whimsical colors make Commander's Palace a geographic as well as culinary landmark

Commander's Palace

CHAPTER ONE

GRACING THE GARDEN DISTRICT

A fine dining joint." That's how Ti Martin describes Commander's Palace, the New Orleans restaurant that her mother, Ella Brennan, and Ella's siblings purchased in 1969. It is fine dining, absolutely, but *joint?* Commander's Palace has a loyal following both locally and nationally and has earned many prestigious dining awards.

Ti explains. "Of course we have standards of professionalism, but a joint is a place where you can feel comfortable. When you see the aqua blue building with the striped awning, you know we don't take ourselves too seriously."

The view expressed by Ti (short for *petit* and pronounced tee) reveals much about Commander's Palace and about the Brennan clan. Ella Brennan couldn't be more serious when she says, "We set out to be the best, not just in New Orleans, but in the country." From the first, she and her siblings exuded a passion for perfecting the entire dining experience, from food to service to decor. They have instilled that passion in their children and in their staff as well so that everyone at Commander's is constantly striving to excel.

But they also want their patrons to relax and

"We set out to be the best, not just in New Orleans, but in the country."—*Ella Brennan*

enjoy themselves, just as they want to enjoy being hosts. The result is that Commander's Palace is the elegant-but-unstuffy restaurant where people go for fun as well as for the fine food; where they go when it is a special occasion or when they just want to make the occasion special.

You know you're in for something different as soon as you arrive at the corner of Washington Avenue and Coliseum Street in the New Orleans Garden District, a cab ride away from the blare and bustle of the French Quarter. You find yourself in a quiet neighborhood and see the blue Victorian mansion with its turrets and dormer windows, its columns and gingerbread trim, its balconies and, yes, the blue-and-white-striped awning. The architectural style is what Ella's sister Dottie Brennan-Bridgeman describes as "Victorian cuckoo."

Then there's the location, across the street from the historic Lafayette Cemetery. In a TV commercial made for American Express some years back, Ella quipped, "We are across the street from a cemetery. That is not wise. There's no such thing as walk-in traffic."

Well, not quite. Novelist Anne Rice, a Garden District resident and author of *Interview with the Vampire* and other books that deal with the occult, has often said that Commander's Palace is her favorite restaurant. She also makes it the favorite of the Mayfair witch family, central characters in many of her novels. In a scene in *The Witching Hour*, the Mayfair

When executive chef Jamie Shannon isn't cooking up a storm at Commander's Palace, he likes to rev up his Harley-Davidson.

witches conduct a burial ceremony in Lafayette Cemetery, then walk into Commander's for a celebratory dinner.

All that aside, Commander's Palace in many ways is still a local restaurant despite its national reputation, and that's the way the Brennans want it. Says Ti, "The people who keep us on our toes are the locals. We know that if we're making them happy, we don't have to worry about much else. So we want them here every day." But there's another reason, she says: "Tourists don't want to come to a tourist-only restaurant."

Ti's cousin Lally Brennan (the two, along with cousin Brad Brennan, are the managing partners of Commander's) voices a similar sentiment. "We target our local people," she says. "You want good word of mouth, so we hold back tables for the locals. We never tell them there's no table."

There's almost always a party going on at Commander's. On New Year's Eve, patrons love to pop the toy champagne bottles and watch confetti come flying out. For Mardi Gras, the ceiling of the entry foyer is crammed with balloons trailing ribbons long enough to reach an adult's waist; arriving guests walk through a jungle of ribbons. If it is your own private celebration, your table can be striped with brightly colored fabric and there'll be a paper chef's hat for the guest of honor.

Guests who step out onto the balcony, at left, have a most unusual view: Lafayette Cemetery, above.

Then there are the special-menu events. A breathtaking Happy Birthday Julia Child! dinner began with a foie gras and truffle terrine served with shiitake carpaccio and touched with a chive-infused dressing. It went on to quail consommé served with a smoked grilled quail breast, Plaquemine Parish field peas, a *brunoise* of Creole vegetables, and garnish of poached quail egg. The eating got serious with the arrival of Pointe à La

Elegant Rooms
To Suit Any Mood

Dining room manager Laura Bright Moore takes guests' orders in the Parlor Room, whose elegance belies its slightly shady past.

"Some people like to be seen, so we seat them in the Garden Room or the main dining room," says Lally Brennan. "If they are locals, it usually turns into a party atmosphere." People in the main dining room are definitely in the spotlight. Guests arriving at the maître d's station can't help but look through the window wall that provides a panoramic view of the diners. This is the most understated of all the rooms in the restaurant, with decor that does not detract from people who want to be the center of attention. Dark moldings and paintings of egrets and herons in neutral tones create a clubby ambience.

The restaurant's other favored location is the Garden Room on the second floor. In this fantasy setting, enormous branches of a 200-year-old live oak wrap around the glass-walled corner, giving the illusion that you are dining in a tree house.

Somehow, Commander's manages to have intimate settings as well. One is an alcove, formed by one of the building's turrets, that is just large enough for a table for four. Another is the Little Room, which can be set with either a single banquet table or four smaller ones. French doors open onto a balcony overlooking Lafayette Cemetery.

Across the Garden Room foyer is the Parlor Room, its walls painted a color that is salmon-pink by day but at night becomes a shade that Dottie Brennan-Bridgeman calls "firecracker red." It exemplifies the contrast that is Commander's Palace. A crystal chandelier and etched-glass hurricane-shade sconces provide the elegance. But on one wall is an enormous triple mirror, its center panel framed with larger-than-life sculptures of voluptuous semiclad females, reminders of the restaurant's past as a haunt of Prohibition-era riverboat captains and "sporting gentlemen."

No tuxedoed captains here. The Brennans don't want their guests intimidated by a staff that is dressed better than they are.

Hache jumbo lump crab meat and Louisiana-raised redfish Napoleon touched with a Honey Island Swamp chanterelle sauce. This was followed by roasted rack of morel-crusted wild boar, served with pineapple, green peppercorn glaze, and a Creole vegetable lasagna. To top it off: white chocolate fig tart with a fig

Managing partners Ti Martin, Brad Brennan, and Lally Brennan continue to burnish Commander's reputation.

brulée. Events like these are open to the public, and "they sell out real fast," says executive chef Jamie Shannon.

Still, it is the regular menu that accounts for the restaurant's following and fame. There are such traditional Commander's Palace favorites as turtle soup *au sherry* and veal chop Tchoupitoulas, grilled and presented with goat cheese-thyme grits and wild mushroom woodland sauce. Or the roasted Mississippi quail, boned and filled with Creole crawfish sausage, served with a sauté of corn and jalapeño and touched with a reduced port quail glaze. Chef Shannon has a number of his own delectable specials, such as the Colorado lamb quartet, with a lamb T-bone, a lamb and Stilton *crepinette,* grilled leg of lamb, and lamb debris in a buttermilk biscuit, all fin-

■
Lunch on the Garden Patio offers a respite from the workaday world.

ished with a minted Madeira sauce accompanied by a sunflower sprout, cucumber, and mizuna salad.

The service at Commander's matches the menu in tone and quality. Each time a course is ready, a troop of waiters materializes, one per diner, and people are served simultaneously. It is that high standard of professionalism again, but with a difference: There is no choreographed lifting of silver domes. That would be too much of an affectation for a "joint." The philosophy is ingrained in every aspect of the restaurant, including the way the dining room staff is dressed. No tuxedoed captains here. The Brennans don't want their guests intimidated by a staff that is dressed better than they are.

That doesn't mean that there is an anything-goes dress code, however.

"We try to be a little dressier here than in the French Quarter," says Lally. "Our customers demand it." This is, after all, the upscale Garden District. So men must wear jackets at dinner and at the jazz brunch, and they generally wear them at lunch as well.

The staff's attire could serve as a metaphor for the contrasts that give Commander's its unusual atmosphere. Brad Brennan, for example, dresses in impeccable taste, pressed and polished, spruced and shining. But his socks might be printed with grapes, with footballs and basketballs, or (his favorites) chili peppers. "You have to be a little colorful," he says.

At once world-class and unpretentious, Commander's blends comfortably with its quiet surroundings. The delightful Garden Patio is reached by walking through the hubbub of the kitchen. The patio, with umbrella-shaded tables, is surrounded by live oak trees, ferns, and flowers. At its far end is the Patio Room with its own glass-enclosed garden. The trees and shrubs were left undisturbed when the room was constructed around them.

A short walkway leads to another patio, lush with trees and plants, bamboo and ferns, azaleas, and Japanese holly. There are carved-stone cherubs along the walkways and a couple of seating areas with stone or wrought-iron benches. Ella and Dottie, both widowed, live in a grand mansion next door and this, in effect, is their back yard. But there is no gate and no "Private Property" sign. Diners may "mosey over" if they want to, says Lally, and the waitstaff are welcome to relax there for a few minutes before beginning work. After all, Commander's is part of the neighborhood.

Spicy aromas waft through the kitchen as chef Shannon sautées juicy Creole tomatoes.

Three generations of Brennans gather for Christmas in 1953. Back row: John Brennan; Ralph Alexis (a family friend); Owen E. Brennan, Jr.; Owen E. Brennan, Sr.; Owen P. Brennan; John Brennan's wife, Claire; Dick Brennan, Sr. Middle row: Dottie Brennan's husband, Ben Bridgeman; Adelaide Brennan; Owen P.'s wife, Nellie; Owen E.'s son, Jimmy; Owen E.'s wife, Maude; Ella Brennan. Front row: Dottie Brennan-Bridgeman; Dick Brennan, Sr.'s wife, Lynne, holding John's son, Ralph; Owen E.'s son Teddy.

THE FIRST FAMILY OF NEW ORLEANS RESTAURANTS

Few people in New Orleans can remember a time when there was no restaurant run by the Brennans. The family has been in the business there for more than half a century. At Commander's Palace, the current management team—Lally Brennan, Ti Adelaide Martin, and Brad Brennan—is the third generation of Brennan restaurateurs. Lally, Ti, Brad, and several of their cousins have either worked at other Brennan-owned restaurants before coming to Commander's, or have worked at Commander's before moving to other family members' restaurants or launching new ones, or. . . But we're getting ahead of the story.

Owen P. Brennan and his eldest son, Owen E. Brennan, Sr., established the Brennans' first restaurant on Bourbon Street in 1946. They named it Vieux Carré, or French

It is a close-knit family and the relatives move around continually, working with and for others as they are needed at their other restaurants.

Quarter, underlining their presence in New Orleans' most famous district. When the Bourbon Street lease expired in 1956, the restaurant relocated to its present Royal Street site and was renamed Brennan's. For many years thereafter, the restaurant was operated by Owen E. and his siblings, John, Ella, Adelaide, Dick, and Dottie.

In 1969, the family bought Commander's Palace, a long-established restaurant in the city's upscale Garden District. They all remained at Brennan's, however, leaving Commander's in the hands of other managers.

Then, in 1974, there was a family disagreement. Under the terms of a settlement, Owen E.'s widow and their children retained ownership of Brennan's. Commander's Palace became the property of the other five siblings, who then took over the on-site supervision of the restaurant. And not a moment too soon. Commander's had declined, and it would be a big job to restore its luster.

Although each of the five siblings played a part in reviving Commander's and turning it into a world-class restaurant, the most visible members of the management team were Dick and Ella. Adelaide died in 1983 and John in 1998. Dick has moved on to other Brennan enterprises, but Ella, still very much involved with the restaurant, commutes across the patio from her house next door. Dottie, who lives with her, is retired but enjoys being close to the enterprise she helped to build.

Ella is the people person, the role model, the motivator. "Mom makes people believe they can do more than they think they can," says Ti.

Operations manager Steve Woodruff agrees. "Ella has a Ph.D. in people," he says. "She wants to see everyone here learn and grow; she truly believes that they can accomplish wonderful things. Saturday afternoons seem to be the time Ella grabs people and works on them—there are no interruptions from the business office." Woodruff speaks from personal experience. When he first came to Commander's, he worked on Saturdays. "I could always plan on spending an hour with Ella."

Naturally, Ella often has dinner at Commander's. She prefers to sit in the main

At left, Dick Brennan, Sr. appraises the work of Gus Martin, chef at the Palace Café. The restaurant is operated by son Dickie Brennan, who looks on approvingly.

Above, Lally Brennan greets one of Commander's longtime customers. On the wall behind her, the three James Beard Foundation awards.

THE COMMANDER'S PALACE BRENNANS

The "Aunts and Uncles"...				
John	Ella	Adelaide	Dick	Dottie
...AND THEIR CHILDREN				
Ralph	Alex		Lauren	Brad
Lally	Ti Adelaide		Dickie	
Cindy				

When the Brennans assumed on-site management of Commander's Palace in 1974, it was supervised by the five Brennan siblings. Later, their children became involved in varying degrees. In the late 1990s, Brad, Lally, and Ti Adelaide were named managing partners.

Among the older generation, Dick proved to be the innovator, the trend-setting originator of the jazz brunch, trout pecan, and bread pudding soufflé. In addition, he has been a leader in his community and in the restaurant industry. While still at Brennan's on Royal Street, Dick, who is a member of the Louisiana Restaurant Association's Hall of Fame, helped persuade the organizers of the Travel Holiday Awards competition, now the DiRōNA Awards, to hold the awards ceremony in New Orleans. He knew that the gathering of restaurant and food industry personalities would attract extensive media coverage, and he saw it as an opportunity to show-case his city's culinary and cultural traditions.

At Commander's, Dick was a hands-on manager. "He would walk into every dining room and look down, checking for spots on the carpet, and up, to see if any light bulbs were out," says Steve Woodruff, operations manager. "Then he'd go into the kitchen and taste everything. He didn't have to do that; he paid people to do that. But his name was on it."

No longer part of the Commander's team, Dick is involved in three restaurants run by other members of the family: Mr. B's Bistro, the Palace Café, and Dickie Brennan's Steakhouse. Officially, he is semiretired, but he is still the eagle-eyed perfectionist. At dinner at the Palace Café one evening, a waiter sets water glasses on the table. Dick reaches over and moves his glass half an inch. Now the placement is correct.

Dick Brennan, Sr., a culinary innovator and an industry leader, is a role model for the next generation of Brennan restaurateurs.

dining room, because "I can see people coming in the front door, see the kitchen, see the pace. If I'm [dining] upstairs, I'm cut off from everything."

She can see people, *and* they can see her. There is a stream of table-hoppers stopping by: people she knows well, people she hasn't seen in years, people she's never seen before. "I recognized you right away," says a camera-toting diner from out of state. The woman tells Ella how much she looked forward to—and how much she enjoyed—her first visit to Commander's.

Ella is still the queen of the Palace, though she'll deny it. "You can leave us out" of this book, she says, indicating herself and Dottie, who is seated nearby. "Focus on the younger generation."

As the eight cousins in the next generation have opened their own restaurants, it has become difficult for observers to keep track of who is where and with whom. It is a close-knit family (the Palace Café originally was to be named Cousins), and the relatives move around continually, working with and for others as they are needed. In addition, outsiders still find it hard to comprehend that the Brennan's restaurant in Houston belongs to the Commander's Palace branch of the family and is not affiliated with the Brennan's on Royal Street.

On site at Commander's, it is equally difficult to pin down the reporting relationships and the areas of responsibility of each family member. When Woodruff first joined the staff, "I felt somewhat overwhelmed on a regular basis," he says. "The structure can't be pigeonholed."

In the late 1990s, as part of the family's estate-planning process, business relationships were realigned. This put the restaurant under the direction of three managing partners, all children of the fifties and sixties. They are John's daughter Lally; Ella's daughter Ti Adelaide (she is named for her aunt Adelaide); and Dottie's son, Brad. Three other cousins head their own restaurant companies.

Lally came to Commander's in 1980 as managing partner. Prior to that, she had helped start Mr. B's Bistro in the French Quarter. Today Mr. B's is managed by Lally's sister, Cindy; Dick Brennan; and his son, Dick, Jr., known as Dickie.

As the cousin with the longest tenure at Commander's, Lally is largely responsible for day-to-day organization. That means coordinating the efforts of operations manager Woodruff, general manager Richard Shakespeare, and executive chef Jamie Shannon. She also handles every-

Dottie Brennan-Bridgeman, left, helps give Commander's Palace its style and flair. Her sister, Ella Brennan, mentors and motivates a staff committed to service.

Lally Brennan and Jamie Shannon have as much fun working at Commander's as their guests have dining there.

"When you work in a family business, you do whatever it takes."
—Lally Brennan

thing that could be considered marketing, advertising, or public relations, plus a lot more.

"When you work in a family business," says Lally, "you do whatever it takes." An enormous bin of oyster shells is needed for a photo shoot; she unhesitatingly hefts the bin until Shannon rushes to her rescue. She is sometimes seen clearing dirty dishes from a table. "If the dishwasher doesn't show up, I'll go into the kitchen and wash dishes," she says. Dashing across the Garden Patio, she swoops down and, without breaking her stride, picks up an errant scrap of paper. To other eyes, it was barely noticeable. Says Lally, "It was screaming at me."

Ella has remarked that Lally is taking over the people part of her job, and it is easy to see why. Ebullient, accommodating, Lally has a nonstop sparkle that is not forced. At lunch one day, when she is the one being visited by a table-hopper, she graciously introduces her dining companion, a businessperson she has just met, as "my friend."

Lally's cousin Ti, an MBA graduate of Tulane University, has a shrewd business sense and an offbeat sense of humor. Prior to joining her family's restaurant business, she launched her own food products company, Creole Cravings. The product line included soups, seasonings, condiments, and a Creole mayonnaise that won a national competition for new products. Ti sold the enterprise to spice giant McCormick & Co. in March 1991.

Ti's restaurant experience began when, at age ten, she was charged with stamping "souvenir" on Commander's Palace menus. While still in high school, she "worked the front door" as maître d' three nights a week. After selling her food company, she joined cousins Dickie and Brad to open the Palace Café.

Since arriving at Commander's in 1998 as a managing partner, Ti has come to focus on the restaurant's new businesses. She has opened a retail

Palace Café, managed by Dick Brennan, Sr., and his children, Dickie and Lauren, is modeled after a French bistro.

food outlet, Foodies Kitchen, in suburban Metairie; she is writing a new Commander's Palace cookbook, and she is helping with the business plan for the new Commander's in Las Vegas. So intensive is Ti's involvement with these projects that she called on her mother, Ella, to forsake semiretirement and assume some of her on-site management duties.

Ti envisioned Foodies Kitchen as a combination of Balducci's, a New York City gourmet shop that also sells prepared foods, and Solari's, an upscale market formerly on the site now occupied by Mr. B's Bistro. She emphasizes that it is *not* fashioned after the now-shuttered Eatzi's food market at Macy's in New York City, which she describes as "slick—the Banana Republic of food." Foodies is "more real, more funky," says Ti, noting that it is a realization of one of Ella's dreams: "Mom always wanted to do something like Harrods," the London department store known for the dazzling displays in its food halls.

What has Foodies to do with Commander's? Ti says her mission is to rescue people from having to eat fast food on their non-Commander's nights. Foodies' customers can buy either raw ingredients or gourmet meals they need simply warm up. The food is of restaurant quality, and the ingredients are purchased from many of the same suppliers used by Commander's.

The cookbook, which Ti is developing with chef Shannon, will have about 200 recipes. No more than a dozen of them will be repeats from *The Commander's Palace New Orleans Cookbook*, by Ella and Dick, which was published in 1984. "I'm technically writing the book," says Ti, "but Lally was involved in starting it and is pulling it all together."

It is possible that Dottie's son Brad (officially Bradford) beat Ti's record for an early start in the business. He began "working" at Commander's, he says, when the Brennans took over the on-site management in 1974. He was nine years old. "Mom was working the front door and would have me seat people," he says. "There was this little kid in a suit showing people to their table." No doubt that charmed the guests, but it also kept costs down in the difficult early days.

While still in his teens, Brad spent time in the kitchen at Mr. B's Bistro learning to prepare appetizers and desserts, then at Commander's under then-executive chef Emeril Lagasse and Shannon, who was executive sous-chef. Says Brad of Lagasse, "He put me through the wringer," an experience that later stood the young man in good stead working in restaurants in Chicago and San Francisco.

At Ella's behest, Brad returned to New Orleans in 1991 to join Ti and Dickie in opening the Palace Café. He stayed with them for about four years, but then it was time to pursue other goals. "I came back to Commander's Palace to learn everything, from warewasher up to a Brennan position," he says. "Because I'm the youngest, the hurdles are highest. I wanted the family to have confidence in me so that if a new restaurant opened, I could do it."

The move brought him the education he sought. "I probably spent longest as kitchen manager because I loved it so much," he says. "The kitchen manager gets everything started in the morning: makes sure the cooks are ready, the staff has supplies, the dining rooms are clean. He's the first one in and the last one out."

It was another four years before Brad reached his ultimate goal. He moved to Las Vegas, where he and his cousin Alex Brennan-Martin, Ella's son, opened a Commander's Palace restaurant in the Aladdin Hotel in the summer of 2000. (Alex continues to live in Houston, where he is managing partner at Brennan's restaurant.) In typical a-Brennan-works-on-everything fashion, Lally and Dottie developed the design concept and menus for the new restaurant.

Thus this generation of Brennan restaurateurs continues the Commander's Palace tradition that, for them, began in 1969. The history of Commander's Palace, however, goes back to the 19th century, as we shall see.

A stone walkway winds through the lush garden that is Ella Brennan and Dottie Brennan-Bridgeman's "back yard."

Ella Brennan and Dottie Brennan-Bridgeman
share a grand old house right next door to
Commander's Palace.

Commander's Palace

CHAPTER THREE

THE STEEP CLIMB TO SUCCESS

*L*aissez les bon temps rouler." This local mantra ("Let the good times roll") may have captured the popular imagination, but visitors discover another New Orleans when they drop by Commander's Palace. True, the good times still roll in the French Quarter, where the Brennan business originated. In Jackson Square, you can listen to impromptu jazz concerts or have your portrait done in charcoal. You can take carriage rides through the narrow streets or wander into historic courtyards and alleyways, shop for antiques or tacky souvenirs, dine in fine restaurants or party in the raucous clubs along Bourbon Street.

But a short taxi ride will bring you to the elegant Garden District, where moneyed businessmen built their stately homes in the mid-19th century. Thirty-room mansions with dramatic two-story porticos are surrounded by elaborate wrought-iron fences and bedecked with ornate exterior moldings and stained glass windows. Broad, serene streets are lined with palm trees, magnolias, and live oaks that arch over the roadway.

In one of these splendid mansions Emile Commander in 1883 opened a restaurant for the wealthy residents of the district. By 1900, Commander's Palace had developed a reputation for fine dining, and for several years it attracted discerning diners from around the world.

It came under new ownership, however, and during the Prohibition era became more infamous than famous. It was a favorite of riverboat captains and sporting gentlemen, accompanied by their ladies of the hour, who used a discreet side entrance, now walled over, to access the private dining rooms upstairs. What tales could be told by the two glossy-white nude sculptures in the Parlor Room!

Respectable families continued to frequent the restaurant during that period, even coming for dinner after church. They used the main entrance. No doubt they relished getting so close to wickedness while maintaining their propriety.

In 1944, the restaurant changed hands again. The new owners, Frank and Elinor Moran, set out to refurbish everything, including the restaurant's reputation. They added the patio and gardens and upgraded the menu. When her husband died, however, Elinor Moran found the task of maintaining the restaurant daunting. She decided to sell.

Location was the chief reason that Commander's appealed to the Brennans. "The whole point was that it *wasn't* in the Quarter," says Ella Brennan. "It would be a Garden District restaurant." That meant that the ambience, menu, and service would be upscale. But the Brennans had miles to go before Commander's would be the kind of restaurant they envisioned. "It took about three years to get financially rolling and another two before we started to climb up that ladder," says Ella.

Her daughter, Ti, attests to that. "There were hard times here when we were little kids," she recalls. "Commander's Palace was a failure when we took it over. But Mom said we had to make it. We had no choice. Everything was on the line."

Seeing Commander's Palace today, it is difficult to imagine that it was ever a failure. Yet knowing that the restaurant—and the

A discreet side entrance,
now walled over,
once was used by
"sporting gentlemen"
and their ladies.

▬

*Top left: The warm, clublike bar at Dickie Brennan's
Steakhouse. Top right: A Victorian lantern lights the
way to Commander's Palace. Bottom left: The view of
Commander's Palace is neatly framed by the tombs in
Lafayette Cemetery. Bottom right: Painted silk lamp-
shades and interior gates grace Bacco.*

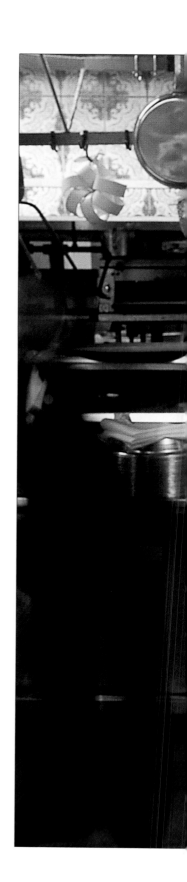

family—went through hard times makes the ascent all the more impressive.

The new managers completely changed the appearance of Commander's. The interior had been Victorian: red flocked wallpaper, gaslit brass chandeliers, dark furniture, dark moldings. Under Dottie and Adelaide's guidance, it was redone in light, bright colors. With trepidation, they accepted a designer friend's suggestion to repaint the outside turquoise, assuredly outré for the neighborhood. Fortunately, the garish color has not only weathered well but also helped make Commander's a geographic, as well as a culinary, landmark.

Inside, there were two significant design changes. On the second floor was a locker room for the staff. One day John looked through the one tiny window in that room and saw the patio, the gardens, and centuries-old live oaks. He also saw potential. "Two days later the walls started coming down," recalls Dottie. The locker room was transformed into the Garden Room. Now, two glass walls offer diners expansive views of the oaks; the open Garden Patio, used as a dining area for six weeks in the spring and six in the fall; and the glass-walled Patio Room, which operates year-round. To add to the illusion of being outdoors, white-painted trellises line the Garden Room walls and ceiling, and there are dramatic floral watercolors on the walls.

The other major alteration was the placement of the bar. "In our first restaurant on Bourbon Street, the bar was in the kitchen," says Dottie. "It was so popular that we decided to do the same thing here." Dick Brennan, who had studied engineering, was heavily involved in the kitchen layout. The configuration entailed a calculated risk. To reach either the bar or the patio, guests must walk through the kitchen.

Top left: The shadowy streets of the French Quarter at night. Above: Guests walk right through the kitchen to reach either the bar or the Garden Patio at Commander's.

An Overflowing Source of Culinary Talent

Brennan's in Houston was opened in 1967 by Jimmy Brennan, a son of Owen E. Brennan, Sr., When the family assets were divided in 1974, ownership went to the Commander's Brennans. Ella's son Alex Brennan-Martin has been at the Houston restaurant since 1983 and is currently managing partner.

Alex is also working with his cousin Brad at the new Commander's Palace in Las Vegas. "It's not a direct copy of Commander's in New Orleans," says Alex, "but the look and feel convey the ambience of New Orleans. It has some age and character built in. We don't have the luxury of 200-year-old oak trees, but we do have a Garden Room."

Besides setting an example for half a dozen other restaurants run by the family, Commander's has helped launch the careers of many chefs who went on to run their own outstanding restaurants. According to an article in the New Orleans *Times-Picayune*, "the kitchen at Commander's Palace has functioned as a kind of New Orleans culinary academy, turning out more than two dozen of the city's finest chefs."

Probably the highest profile graduates of that culinary academy are Paul Prudhomme, executive chef from 1975 to 1980, and Emeril Lagasse, executive chef from 1982 to 1989. Praising the Brennans' business acumen, Prudhomme says, "We helped each other. I was a good cook. I helped build their business and they taught me how to make money running a restaurant. I'd had my own restaurants before. Four were failures and the next three were successes. The Brennans helped me understand that you could appreciate making money as well as making great food."

Prudhomme was an apt pupil. He now has a business empire of his own that includes, in addition to the renowned K-Paul's Louisiana Kitchen in New Orleans, his own line of herbs and spices, a meat processing plant producing seasoned and smoked meats, and a mail order company.

Lagasse, high-voltage star of two shows on the TV Food Network and author of several books, has three restaurants in New Orleans, two in Las Vegas, and one in Orlando, Florida.

Among the other New Orleans restaurateurs trained or influenced by Commander's are Frank Brigtsen and Anne Kearney. Brigtsen, who served under Prudhomme in 1978 and 1979, is chef-owner of Brigtsen's restaurant and in 1998 received the James Beard award for Best Chef in the Southeast. Kearney, who worked at one of Lagasse's restaurants, is chef-owner of Peristyle. She was among those who competed against Commander's Jamie Shannon when he won the James Beard award for Best Chef in the Southeast in 1999.

The list goes on, evidence that Commander's Palace, besides making its own mark in the restaurant world, has had an incalculable influence on other outstanding restaurants.

Newer Brennan Restaurants and Their Managers

Ralph Brennan Restaurant Group			Dickie Brennan & Co.		Owned Jointly
Bacco	*Red Fish Grill*	*Storyville District*	*Palace Café*	*Dickie Brennan's Steakhouse*	*Mr. B's Bistro*
Ralph	Ralph	Ralph	Dick	Dickie	Ralph
			Dickie	Lauren	Dickie
			Lauren		Cindy

The glass-walled Patio Room is popular for private parties. Below: Brennan's in Houston is managed by Ella Brennan's son, Alex Brennan-Martin.

Although visitors are fascinated by this peek behind the scenes, the ready access requires that the executive chef and his staff not be rattled when strangers wander through.

Physical changes were just the beginning. Talented chefs were hired, the menu was revamped, and the Brennans began to introduce their personal philosophy of fine service. As the restaurant grew, the standards were set higher and higher.

Having learned the risks of absentee management, they developed the BOD (Brennan on Duty) schedule, which ensures that there is at least one member of the family present when the restaurant is open. "It's like entertaining in your home," says Lally. "When you have a guest, you're there."

Now the challenge was to find a way to bring back disaffected customers and show them the new

*Dining in the Garden Room gives the
illusion of being in a treehouse.*

Commander's proved an industry leader when other restaurants emulated its Sunday jazz brunch.

Commander's Palace. There needed to be a powerful drawing card. On Royal Street, "We had hung our hat on Breakfast at Brennan's," says Ella. "That distinguished the restaurant." Breakfast at Brennan's became a tradition, an institution, for locals and for visitors. What could Commander's do that would be equally distinctive?

While on a trip to London, Dick had an inspiration. Legend has it he was so excited he phoned Ella immediately to tell her his idea: a Sunday jazz brunch with a strolling Dixieland band entertaining patrons while they dined. Ella's response: Why didn't we ever think of this before?

The jazz brunch clicked immediately. Business was so brisk the restaurant suddenly was short-staffed. Dick's son, Dickie, was pressed into service as a busboy—"his first real job," muses Dick.

Several other restaurants in New Orleans were soon to follow with jazz brunches of their own.

Commander's jazz brunch has become so popular that it is held on Saturday as well as Sunday. It is a festive affair, with orange, green, yellow, red, blue, and white balloons tied to the chair backs in all the dining rooms. Bassist Joe Simon's jazz trio has performed at the brunches since the 1980s.

The success of the jazz brunch meant that the locals knew Commander's was back. But the Brennans wanted more than a strong local reputation. They had set their sights on expanding their clientele, but there was no plan for realizing that goal.

Inspiration came during the American Cuisine Symposium that the managers attended in Louisville, Kentucky. "Nouvelle cuisine had come upon the scene," says Ella, "and the country was just beginning to respect chefs. At the

Ralph Brennan's newest venture, Storyville District restaurant and nightclub.

symposium, there were lots of panel discussions; everyone was interested in what others were doing." Attendees were so enthusiastic that they wanted to schedule another symposium, so the publicity-savvy Brennans invited them to New Orleans.

On the final night of the next symposium, in 1983, Commander's Palace was closed to the public and the Brennans hosted a dinner for the attendees. "People were thrilled beyond words," says Ella. "That was the beginning of Commander's Palace being recognized by people outside the city. We set out to be the best restaurant not just in New Orleans but in the country."

They achieved their goals. The high point came in 1996, when the James Beard Foundation honored Commander's with its Outstanding Restaurant Award for best restaurant in the country. The management team is also proud that Commander's has been voted New Orleans' most popular restaurant in the *Zagat Survey* every year since Zagat began reporting on the city in 1988.

As Commander's reputation grew, so did the next generation of Brennans. Several of them wanted to follow in their parents' footsteps. Soon New Orleans' First Family of Restaurants was giving birth to a family of restaurants.

Today, there are six restaurants in New Orleans owned or managed by the younger generation of Brennans. John's son, Ralph, heads Ralph Brennan Restaurant Group, which includes Mr. B's Bistro, Bacco, Red Fish Grill, and Storyville District.

Ralph's sister, Cindy, manages Mr. B's Bistro, which, in a familial arrangement, is owned jointly by Ralph's group and Dickie Brennan & Co. Dickie, son of Dick, trained under chef Paul Prudhomme at Commander's and later spent two years as managing partner there. In addition to sharing Mr. B's Bistro, his group includes Palace Café and Dickie Brennan's Steakhouse. Dickie's sister, Lauren, who was at Commander's from 1985 to 1991, is a partner at Palace Café and at Dickie Brennan's Steakhouse.

A simple ironwork gate leads into the Garden Patio.

The "Patio Food" menu offers entrées that are a tad lighter but just as attractive and flavorful.

Commander's Palace

CHAPTER FOUR

A PHILOSOPHY THAT REWRITES THE RULES

On a wall in the kitchen at Commander's Palace is a framed motto that reads, "Commander's Golden Rule: Treat the customer as the customer wants to be treated."

Yes, Commander's Palace has rewritten the Golden Rule, perhaps because there is a touch of arrogance in "Do unto others as you would have them do unto you." Why should people assume that everyone else wants to be treated the same way they do? The Brennans are insightful enough to know better. They have turned the maxim around and are putting others first.

COMMANDER'S GOLDEN RULE
"Treat the Customer as the Customer Wants to be Treated"

Treating customers the way they want to be treated, putting them at ease, making them feel welcome and appreciated—that is what Commander's stands for. The food plays an important role in this process, of course. Ella makes that clear when she talks about the evolution of American cuisine and the restaurant's goal of continually creating new and exciting dishes. Top-flight cuisine has built Commander's reputation. It is the reason people go there. But the Brennans know that if the service falls short, people won't come back, regardless of how good the food is.

Still, it is not easy to provide superb service. As Ella puts it, "How can you teach a young server to be gracious but not forward; to have a sense of urgency but to be graceful; to be knowledgeable but unintimidating; to be friendly but professional? Yet that level of finesse is exactly what we must teach them."

It starts, of course, with hiring the right people. "Each department does its own interviewing, hiring, and training," says operations manager Steve Woodruff. "The most important thing is finding people who have the motivation to serve."

Then those people must be trained. But achieving the finesse that Ella describes requires more than just teaching them the correct procedures. It is necessary to communicate the unique Commander's philosophy.

"Very few people have worked at someplace like Commander's," says Woodruff. "Once a month I spend a day with new employees trying to share what our restaurant is about, how we feel about our customers, what lengths we'll go to for them. Some people feel that if they're providing a service, they're in a subservient role."

To help employees understand the value of what they do, Woodruff uses examples from *The Real Heroes of Business . . .and Not a CEO Among Them.* The inspirational book, by Bill Fromm and Len Schlesinger, is in the employee library in one corner of Commander's kitchen. Its heroes include a hotel doorman, an

Chef Paul Prudhomme, one of Commander's best-known alumni.

*Commander's food runners live up
to their name as they speed prepared dishes
from the kitchen to the dining rooms.*

"Gang service," when everyone at the table is served simultaneously, is a Commander's Palace signature.

auto mechanic, and a loan officer. Says Woodruff, "It's about people on the front lines making it happen every day."

But there can be no better example of the philosophy that service is not subservience than the Brennans themselves. Once a year, they host a dinner for the dining room captains, and the meal is served by the family members. "It's a riot!" says Lally. "It's so much fun." Then she adds, "You never know how hard it is until you try to do it." That is how the owners come to understand and appreciate how hard it is to provide the level of service for which Commander's is famous.

General manager Richard Shakespeare, who was hired as a busboy in the 1970s, has his own take on what the Brennans are trying to achieve. "The philosophy the Brennans have is to make this a comfortable, unintimidating place. The ideal is for us to be a glorified bistro."

Putting Commander's Golden Rule into practice, he says, requires that "the dining room manager be able to 'read' the table. Our challenge is to determine if customers want to clown around or be left alone."

On a busy evening, it is possible to see the challenge being met in several different ways. Example: Dining room manager Ray Brinkman notices a patron eating pasta with a fork and asks, "Would you like a spoon? You look like a twirler." The diner laughs and admits that she does prefer to eat pasta by twirling it on a spoon.

With regular customers, of course, there shouldn't be any guesswork. "We need to know what they want, their idiosyncracies," says Shakespeare. "We have one customer who wants his drink fast, wants to get his menu and have his order taken fast, and then he slows right down." That is what the customer wants, the staff knows it, and that is what he gets.

Shakespeare is fond of saying that "a good waiter can save a bad meal, but a good meal can't save a bad waiter." His point is clear, though it is hard to imagine either a bad meal or poor service at Commander's. For one thing, servers undergo rigorous training to provide impeccable, individualized service. For another, they can concentrate on the needs of their customers because they never have to leave to retrieve orders from the kitchen. There is a computer in each dining room, and orders are entered there. Retrieval is handled by entry-level staffers known as runners. Using runners means having another 25 people on the payroll. The Brennans think it is worth the cost because it helps them boost the level of service yet another notch.

There is something else that makes Commander's service extraordinary. In a good restaurant, the waiters remember who ordered what, and they place the food in front of the right people. In a fine restaurant, the waiters also remember to serve women first. But at Commander's Palace, everyone is served at the same time, thanks to a procedure known as "gang service." (The staff is trying to learn to call it "team service," but a mischievous spirit prevails.) This isn't the familiar ritual in which waiters place a dome-topped plate before each diner, reach forward to seize the handle on the dome, then watch for the signal: ready, set, lift!

Despite the name, Commander's gang service is smooth and unobtrusive. There are enough waiters so that when a runner comes in with a tray, the dining room manager can quickly assemble a team, one waiter for each diner, and the food is served to everyone simultaneously.

Like the service, the food is abundant. Ignoring the trend at many upscale restaurants, Commander's believes in serving large portions. That is what customers want, says Ella, but it is also what Commander's wants to give.

People in the restaurant industry are by nature hospitable and giving. Yet the Brennans stand out in many ways. Says alumnus chef Paul Prudhomme, "Whenever I did something with them, a public appearance or an event at the restaurant, I always had anything I need-

▬

*Opposite page, the entrance to
Ella Brennan and Dottie Brennan-
Bridgeman's Garden District
home. Above, chef Shannon sips
a sauce to check the seasoning.
Left, managing partners Ti Martin
and Lally Brennan greet a guest
in the entry foyer.*

ed to make it turn out well. I had as many people, as much product as I needed." He adds, "They operate with lots of finesse and style."

Delores Nenera, a taxi driver who knows the neighborhood, has not dined at Commander's, but she has experienced the spirit of generosity. "When I deliver a heavy package to the restaurant, they tip me," she says. "Most restaurants don't."

This sensitivity to others shows up, too, in the restaurant's attitude toward single diners. In many places, it can be difficult to make a reservation for one person. Articles written for businesspeople traveling alone even suggest making a reservation for two and, on arriving at the restaurant, saying apologetically that the second person couldn't make it.

No such ruse is necessary at Commander's. In fact, when Woodruff is told about the restrictions at other restaurants, his eyes widen in disbelief. "The Brennans want to squelch the aversion to single diners," he says. "We have enough seats so we can accommodate them." There are about 370 seats, mostly tables for four. But throughout the restaurant there are seven tables for two—or one. Single diners even receive a lagniappe (the New Orleans term for a little something extra), usually a complimentary after-dinner drink.

Dottie Brennan-Bridgeman sums it up when she says, "Customers could have gone to dozens of other restaurants, but they chose ours. We're glad they did, and we tell them so."

Above, Commander's is known for serving generous portions.
Above right, the carved stone fountain was installed when
the Garden Patio was remodeled. Below right, Lally Brennan
affectionately greets friends.

"A good waiter can save a bad meal, but a good meal can't save a bad waiter."

—*Richard Shakespeare, general manager*

Ins and Outs of a Family Business

Volumes have been written about what it is like working with family members and what can be done to keep relations harmonious. "We're a perfect example of sometimes it works and sometimes it doesn't," says Lally Brennan, alluding to the dispute that split her family's business in 1974. But the Brennans' philosophy of family management does work at Commander's. There are three cousins on site, two of them accustomed to working with, and for, their mothers. Other cousins have been at the restaurant for extended periods. How do they do it?

Lally:

- "We treat each other with the utmost respect. We're taught that it's okay to disagree, but not to be disagreeable."
- "You have to separate business and play. When we do a family dinner, we make a point of leaving the business at the front door."
- "You have to walk the extra mile to make it work."

Ti:

- "You have to be committed to communicating. It helps if you really like each other, which we do."
- "You have to keep your egos in check. Fortunately, that hasn't been much of a problem around here."
- "We try to be fair and spread the duties around so everyone can have a life."
- "I've always had so much respect for my mother. She won't tell me what to do; we work things out together. And she's a riot to work with; she's so funny!"

Brad:

- "Working with a family member is easier because you have a greater level of trust and you know that you want to take care of each other. But it's harder because you sometimes try to protect them too much, to fill in for them when they have a problem in their personal life."
- "If they're not in favor of an idea, you go out of your way to bring [the family member] on board. And you ask yourself if the idea is really that important to you. The CEO of IBM wouldn't worry about upsetting the chief financial officer or marketing officer the way we'd worry about upsetting a family member. Maybe he should."
- "My mother treats me as a business associate. I feel more of an obligation to do things right because she's a senior partner and she's my mother."
- "Working in a family business conditions you to treat all people like family. You earn their respect that way, you create longevity and growth, and you can go so much farther."

The three cousins say they also have excellent relationships with nonfamily people who have worked at the restaurant for a number of years. "We've come to respect them so much," says Ti. "You get to a point where they feel like adopted family." What is it like when you're not a member of the family? Operations manager Steve Woodruff agrees that the two camps work well together.

Steve Woodruff:

- "This group of siblings had to figure out a way to work together, form a team, and play off each others' strengths. As a natural outcome of that, you see teams and team relationships here."
- "Operations and family people together set the structure of the restaurant."
- "We bounce things off each other and appreciate each others' opinions."

*Snapping a crisp white cloth
onto a table on the Garden Patio.*

Executive chef Jamie Shannon was named Best Chef in the Southeast by the James Beard Foundation. Opposite, Creole vegetables on homemade brioche with sweet potato chips.

Commander's Palace

CHAPTER FIVE

FROM TURTLE SOUP TO LEMON FLAN

Commander's Palace is such a New Orleans tradition that you half expect the menu to be unchanged from the last time you were there, maybe even the same as the day the Brennans moved uptown and assumed management. It will be outstanding, but familiar; just order your meal on autopilot.

Wrong. There is always something innovative, intriguing, irresistible at this landmark restaurant. A number of traditional dishes are on the menu, of course, but they have been updated to bring them in line with culinary trends and people's changing tastes.

Early in their tenure, Ella and Dick Brennan set the example of constant change. The dining public was beginning to show an appreciation for fine food, and the managers seized the opportunity to transform Commander's into a world-class restaurant.

"It was a great time to be creative," recalls Ella. "We were trying to take the best food in New Orleans and bring it into today." They succeeded on several fronts, but especially in providing an atmosphere that

has attracted innovative chefs over the years. The latest is executive chef Jamie (officially James P.) Shannon, who has won a succession of awards for his command of modern Creole cookery.

Shannon deftly balances the traditional and the innovative. Along with the classics are such *au courant* dishes as pan-seared foie gras served with Sauternes gastrique, citrus segments, and grilled home-made bread; and poached jumbo spring asparagus served with a smoked Atlantic salmon and fennel slaw with truffle sherry vinaigrette.

There is an array of popular dishes long identified with the restaurant. As Alex Brennan-Martin says of the menu at the new Commander's Palace in Las Vegas, "It wouldn't be safe to omit turtle soup, trout pecan, and bread pudding soufflé. They are the classics people expect at Commander's."

Trout pecan was conceptualized by Dick Brennan in 1975, the same year he originated the jazz brunch. At the time, many restaurants in New Orleans served trout almondine. Walking from his home to the restaurant every day, Dick passed under rows of pecan trees, their abundance crunching beneath his feet. It suddenly occurred to him that pecans have much more flavor than almonds. And where do the almonds come from anyway, California?

That settled it. "Throw out the almonds!" he told the chef. From then on, Commander's Palace would serve trout pecan. It wasn't long before other restaurants in New Orleans changed their trout almondine to trout pecan. Once again, Commander's had set the standard.

Dick Brennan's original trout pecan was double-battered, pan sautéed, and topped with pecan butter and roasted pecans. The con-temporary version, which is not double battered, is lighter. Instead of a rich sauce, it is served with brown butter with fresh thyme and lemon.

Turtle soup, however, remains unchanged. It is still roux-enriched, thick with turtle meat, and enlivened with a dash of sherry when served.

Then there is the bread pudding soufflé, introduced at the Second American Cuisine Symposium in 1983 and a Commander's signature ever since. For this dessert, the classic New Orleans bread pudding is

*Putting the finishing touches on
rich crème brulée.*

"Throw out the almonds!" Dick Brennan
commanded, and trout pecan was born.

Innovating in a Sumptuous Tradition

The basic orientation of the Commander's Palace menu is Creole, a term that applies to the French and Spanish settlers in New Orleans as well as to their style of cooking. Although there are differences of opinion, Creole is generally considered to be the cooking done in the cities. It is carefully presented and more refined than the rustic Cajun cooking of central Louisiana. Some years back, the Commander's Palace menu carried this explanation of the restaurant's approach to Creole cooking:

"The mere words 'Creole Cuisine' tend to stimulate our appetites. Our taste buds tingle at the very thought of sumptuous servings of salty oysters from the Barataria marshes, blue-claw crabs from Lake Pontchartrain, scarlet crawfish from the Atchafalaya swamps, rich gumbos thickened with pulverized leaves from sassafras trees and those prickly green vegetables from the mirliton vines. With such exotic ingredients, Creole cooks, over the years, have created dishes that are world-renowned.

"Our new Haute Creole Cuisine takes those same luscious ingredients, even some of the same basic recipes, a step further in the continuing evolution of this unique cuisine. The results are dishes that are lighter, more subtle, yet every bit as delicious and exotic."

Chef Jamie Shannon continues in Commander's tradition of updating and lightening dishes. "We don't use as much butter and cream as we used to," he says. "They used to be in almost every sauce. Now we use reductions, marinades, and purees. We might have a mushroom puree or a brandy morel reduction or homemade crème fraîche with Duckhorn Vineyards vermouth. And we cook with different oils; sometimes clarified butter, sometimes olive oil." He cites the crawfish sauté with sweetbreads, which is sauced with a morel brandy and wild mushroom *fonds de veau*, and served on grilled slices of homemade onion bread.

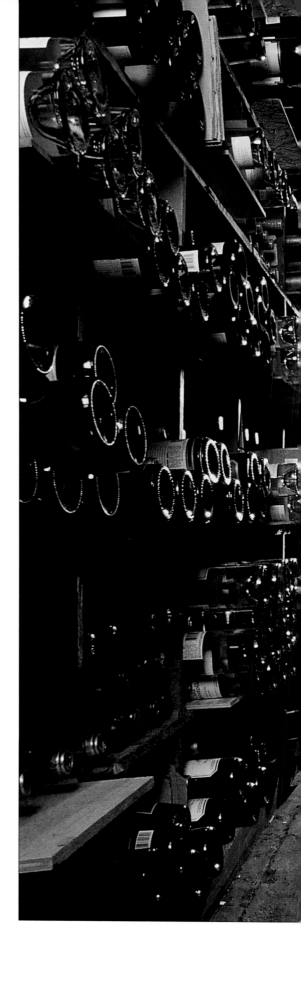

General manager Richard Shakespeare takes stock of Commander's award-winning wine cellar.

frothed into a soufflé and served with a rich sauce of bourbon, sugar, and cream lightly flavored with cinnamon.

Another dish in which Dick Brennan had a hand—more accurately a tasting spoon—is the lemon flan, a sweet-tart custard topped with a thin, crispy sheet of pastry and served with a lemon curd sauce. "It's based on Grandmother Brennan's lemon icebox cake," says Dick's son, Dickie, noting that it took his father six months of experimenting before he was satisfied with the result.

Complementing Commander's menu is a wine list that in 1998 received an Award of Excellence from *Wine Spectator.* The Brennans have long been proponents of California wines, and perhaps 200 of the 500 labels on the wine list are from California. But there are also about 150 from France plus good representation from Germany, Italy, Spain, Australia, New Zealand, Chile, Oregon, and Washington.

Guests are amazed by the diversity of Commander's cuisine. The various presentations for the grilled Gulf fish of the day, for example, include one with a ragout of local legumes topped by a miniature salad of fresh farm herbs and greens in a roasted shallot vinaigrette. Among the newer favorites is Lyonnaise Gulf fish with a crunchy potato crust, served with a fennel cabbage slaw and smoked-tomato sauce, and sparked with a garnish of fried capers.

A New Jersey "Creole" in Commander's Palace

When describing Commander's menu, executive chef Jamie Shannon says, "We stick to our Creole roots," but his own roots are not quite Creole. He was raised in Sea Isle, New Jersey, and his earliest jobs were in a cafeteria and at a seafood restaurant in a neighboring resort town.

Even as a child, Shannon learned to respect fresh local foods. His godfather was a lobster fisherman, and young Jamie often went to the docks to watch the day's catch being unloaded. Fresh pasta and cheese could be purchased from street vendors. In the summer, Shannon visited his great-grandparents, who lived on a farm in nearby Cape May Courthouse. They grew vegetables and herbs, raised chickens and hogs, and made their own sausage.

During his tenure at the seafood house, Shannon decided to make a career of cooking. He applied to the Culinary Institute of America in Hyde Park, New York, and was awarded a full scholarship.

At the CIA, he specialized in American cuisine, and he soon heard of the Brennans' pronouncements that America's most exciting regional cuisine was Creole. His adviser, Tim Ryan, who later became executive vice president at the CIA, suggested that he head for New Orleans.

Shannon came to Commander's just a few months after his graduation in 1984. Emeril Lagasse was Commander's executive chef at the time. Starting as saucier, Shannon moved up through the ranks, eventually becoming executive sous-chef. When Lagasse left in 1990, Shannon was made executive chef. He supervises a kitchen staff of 43 people.

An award-winning chef in an award-winning restaurant, Shannon was proclaimed New Orleans chef of the year in 1992 by Chefs in America (now Awards of the Americas). In 1998, he was named chef of the year by *New Orleans* magazine, and that same year he was featured in the Horchow catalog, which showcased his preparations of seafood gumbo with okra, smoked Gulf fish cakes, and chocolate pralines. Shannon's shining moment, however, came in 1999 when he outscored some impressive competition to win the James Beard Foundation's award for Best Chef in the Southeast.

Commander's kitchen produces several hundred award-winning meals each day.

Freshness of ingredients is paramount. The focus on local seasonal products began prior to Shannon's tenure, but he has expanded it. "A good 70 percent of the menu is indigenous ingredients," he says. Pheasant, quail, rabbit, duck, and venison come from local suppliers, as do soft shell crabs, redfish, crawfish, and fruits and vegetables.

The plump, crisp-fried soft shell crabs, sometimes served atop a grain salad, suddenly appear on thick slices of juicy Creole tomatoes when they're in season. The tomatoes come from farms in the Mississippi delta town of Waggaman. As soon as the strawberries are ripe in Ponchatoula, customers can expect to feast on Commander's own strawberry shortcake, made with a buttermilk biscuit and fresh chantilly cream.

Another specialty is the choupique caviar. In the same family as the American sturgeon, choupique dates back millions of years and is available only in North America. Shannon obtains his choupique caviar either directly from the man who raises the fish and harvests the eggs or from a distributor in New Orleans.

Finding local suppliers requires traveling the countryside, seeking reliable sources, and cultivating relationships with them. Once suppliers are chosen, says Shannon, "we make it easier for them. We pick things up so they

Plump soft shell crabs from local suppliers, crisply fried, are sometimes served with thick slices of creole tomatoes. Bottom right, juicy Ponchatoula strawberries are featured in Commander's strawberry shortcake.

don't have to deliver. There are three people in our purchasing department. One purchases, and two people go pick up things." That is more work than receiving deliveries from a distributor, but it enables Commander's to serve the freshest possible foods.

Using local purveyors requires flexibility. "Sometimes we don't know until a few hours before we open what will be available," Shannon says. It depends, for example, on what the catch of the day happens to be. The other side of the coin is Commander's obligation to use the products. "If we've dedicated ourselves to certain farmers, we have to use what they have," the chef explains.

Local suppliers are so valued that they are identified on the kitchen blackboard where daily specials are listed. Suppliers are also described to the waitstaff at the daily premeal briefing, and many are even listed on the menu: LaFourche redfish; P&J oysters, which the Brennans have purchased for their restaurants for more than 50 years; Chicory Farm cheeses; Duckhorn Vineyards vermouth.

Commander's is also its own supplier. The kitchen makes sausages, terrines, and patés, as well as gravlax, Worcestershire sauce, goat cheese, breads, and, of course, all the desserts. The bake shop has a dessert chef and a crew of eight or nine people making ice cream, sorbets, pies, and Creole cream cheese cake from scratch. Lally Brennan claims that Creole cream cheese, an incredibly rich cheese available only in the New Orleans area, even makes converts of out-of-towners raised to believe that true cheesecake is found only in New York.

Local suppliers provide everything from pheasant, quail, and venison to soft shell crabs and crawfish.

For Ella Brennan and Jamie Shannon,
Commander's haute Creole cuisine is
serious business.

LET THE GOOD TASTES ROLL!

Like any creative chef, Jamie Shannon looks forward to pulling out all the stops. He does so frequently, especially at his chef's table in Commander's kitchen. There, four customers lucky enough to enjoy the privilege can dig into one of his seven-course tasting menus. This is his Creole Louisiana Seafood Tasting Menu:

• P&J hand-selected Black Bay oysters with Creole mustard, green onion mignonette, and choupique caviar;

• Jumbo lump crab cake seared and served with Commander's own ravigote sauce and bell peppers, and finished with a ragout of fresh corn, thyme, and jalapeño;

• Classic New Orleans crawfish bisque, served with a buttermilk cracked-black-pepper biscuit and crawfish tails;

• New Orleans-style barbecue shrimp, served with a spicy garlic rosemary sauce and garlic aïoli French bread;

• Pan-roasted, seared LaFourche redfish and foie gras, served on a bed of roasted local mushrooms, leeks, and Parisienne vegetables, with a light fumet and balsamic reduction;

• Local handmade cheeses from cow, goat, and sheep's milk, served with crispy French bread;

• A Ponchatoula strawberry tasting, consisting of a miniature strawberry shortcake, individual Creole cream cheese strawberry cheesecake, and strawberry ice cream.

Arriving at Commander's:
A memorable evening is about to begin.

Commander's Palace

CHAPTER SIX

YOUR TABLE IS READY

Ruth Rose and Marilyn Lefkowitz have finished lunch at Commander's Palace, and they are glowing. In town on vacation from a suburb of New York City, they are the last people in the main dining room. It is their first time at Commander's, and they can't tear themselves away. Nor can they contain their praise.

"The food is so good, and I've never seen such service!" Ruth exclaims. "We had two waiters bringing our plates. And the waiters are so nice, so polite. I ordered the fried Gulf shrimp salad, and I asked if I could have the shrimp not fried. The waiter said, 'Of course you can; we'll sauté it.' And I find the prices very reasonable."

Marilyn picks up the conversation. "People at home and people who live here told us not to miss this restaurant. This is elegant dining without pretense. You don't have to worry if you are using the wrong fork. You can just relax."

Those are words to warm a Brennan's heart. Ruth and Marilyn have picked up on much of what matters to the management. Little do they realize that they will soon have the opportunity to take their praise right to the top.

As waiter Robert Bertot walks by, Marilyn asks, "Robert, how many dining rooms are there?"

"Would you like to see the rest of the restaurant?" he asks

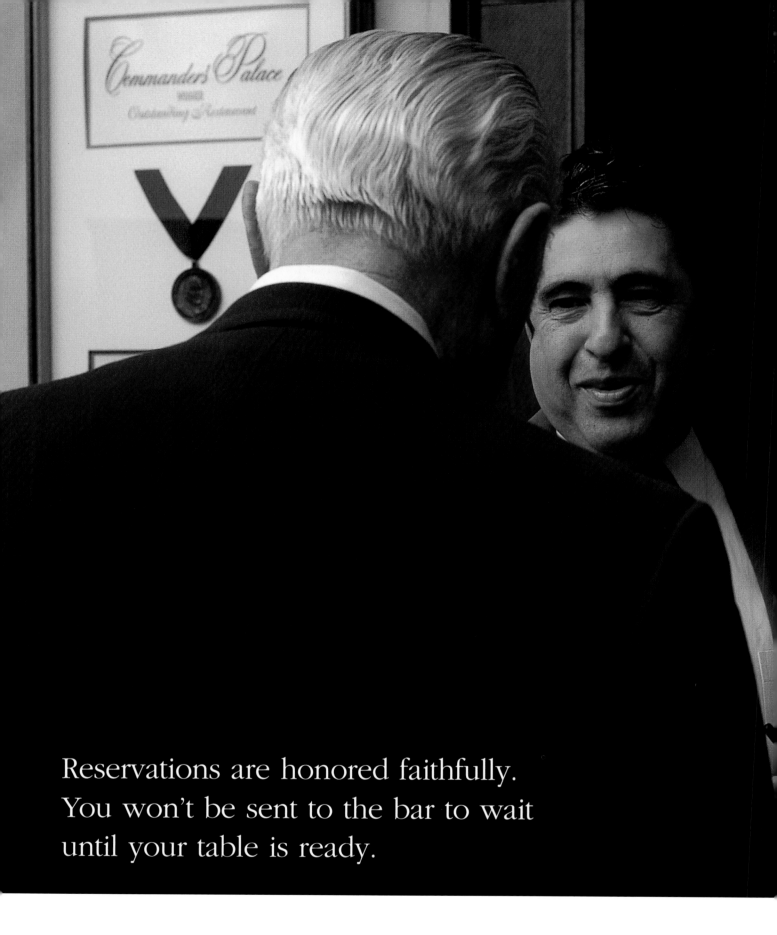

Reservations are honored faithfully.
You won't be sent to the bar to wait
until your table is ready.

Maître d' George Rico has been with Commander's since before the Brennans arrived.

in reply, and the next thing the women know, they are being taken on a private tour.

As they move from room to room, Bertot, obviously well trained, gives them a bit of the history and calls their attention to details of the decor. The women are charmed.

Then, crossing the Garden Patio, the group encounters Ella Brennan. Bertot introduces Ruth and Marilyn, and they describe in effusive terms what a wonderful experience they have had. Ella puts her palms together as if in prayer, smiles, and graciously bows her head to the two women. It is a moment they will never forget. How many of their friends will hear this story and put Commander's Palace on their must-see lists?

Not everyone is lucky enough to get a guided tour, of course, but in many ways the women's experience is typical of what every guest at Commander's can expect: top-flight food, exceptional service, and a staff that provides whatever the customer wants, often before it is requested. All this in a setting that is elegant without being intimidating.

As a guest, you can look forward to another hospitable practice: Your reservation will be honored. You won't be sent to the bar to wait until your table is ready. The bar is where people go for after-dinner drinks.

There was a time, however, when reservations were not always handled so smoothly. "When we started, we knew nothing about reservations," Ella acknowledges. Their savior in those days was her sister Adelaide Brennan.

"Miss Adelaide was a first-class lady," recalls maître d' George Rico, who was hired by Commander's previous owner, Frank Moran, and was a waiter when the Brennans bought the restaurant. "She was the entertainer. If we fell behind in our reservations, we sent people to the bar to wait and Miss Adelaide would talk with them." Adelaide was such an engaging conversationalist that when people's tables were finally ready, they were often reluctant to leave the bar.

THAT MAGIC TOUCH

reparations for a memorable Commander's Palace experience begin the minute a person phones to make a reservation. "We do profiles of people," says Dottie Brennan-Bridgeman. "If you say, for example, that you're coming to celebrate Aunt Mary's 79th birthday, we write that down, and every waiter wishes her a happy birthday. If it's a special occasion, we 'stripe' the table."

The reservations office keeps no secrets. Every staff member who will be involved with your meal knows your name and why you are there. "I see the reservations list every day," says executive chef Jamie Shannon. "If it's a celebration—an anniversary, a first communion, or someone getting engaged—we all say congratulations. We might have balloons at the table or do a special dessert. We want you to know that we're glad you're having a good time and celebrating with us."

Left, a celebration in the Garden Room. Above, Commander's wine list showcases California but also offers a wide range of domestic and international choices.

When you enter Commander's, you will probably be greeted by Rico, who has been with the restaurant since 1962, or perhaps by general manager Richard Shakespeare, who arrived in the late 1970s. You might be shown to your table by a Brennan family member or by an entry-level food runner. There is no hierarchy; the important thing is that you be welcomed and shown to your table immediately. The instant you are seated, you will be served some of Commander's own Parmesan-and-dill-scented garlic bread. It is cut in strips, much neater to eat than rounds.

General manager Richard Shakespeare flames café brûlot.

EGOS CODDLED HERE

At Commander's Palace, special requests are no problem.

During the meal, you will notice other special touches. Water glasses, with plenty of ice in them, will be removed and replaced at least once. If you should leave the table, you will return to find that your napkin has not simply been refolded, which is done in some fine restaurants, but has been replaced with a fresh one, which is rarely done anywhere else.

When the menu arrives, try to restrain yourself for a moment. Turn it over and look first at the artwork. Some years back, the menu was a buff-colored, matte-finish folder printed with greenish-blue ink. Dull. It didn't begin to convey the fun that is such an important part of Commander's.

Today the menus are designed to create a special mood. On the dinner and tasting menus, a sketch in coppery-gold pastels depicts the kitchen in action. The chefs are hustling, but they are not frantic and they are all smiling. The Jazz Brunch menu has a fanciful drawing of a trumpet-playing chef with colorful balloons in the background, lobsters in the foreground, and "Commander's Celebration" in bold script. On the lunch menu, there is a

How does the management at Commander's Palace create an ambience where diners can just relax and have a good time? By never themselves relaxing, by being passionate, even obsessive, about the details.

"We've broken down the dining process, minute by minute," says general manager Richard Shakespeare. "If we have the right interaction, what do we expect to have happen?" That analysis is applied to everything from taking the reservation and how the valet handles the car to how the guests are greeted at the door and how they're seated.

Creating the perfect dining experience is not easy. Shakespeare notes, for example, that "at least 50 percent of people assigned to a table ask to be moved to another. People want to be against the wall, away from the wall. . . ." Whatever patrons want, they get, because "we're in the business of coddling egos."

Waitstaff are expected to address the host of each group of diners by name. That information comes from the reservations office. "If we're doing everything right," says Shakespeare, "we write the host's name on the back of the check and the first person who goes to the table uses the name. That goes back to the philosophy of entertaining someone in your home." It also goes back to the philosophy of attention to detail.

At a pre-meal meeting, chef
Shannon tells the staff which
local products are featured on
the menu.

photograph of enticing entrées arrayed photogenically on a single table on the Garden Patio.

When you open the menu to check the prices, you will be pleasantly surprised. This is a restaurant that has won countless awards for its food and its service, and yet you can order a three-course lunch for $14.50, a three-course brunch for $23 to $29, or a three-course dinner for $32 to $37 (all prices before wine, tax, and tip). The seven-course tasting menu, which often includes caviar, foie gras, and other costly ingredients, is a modest $75.

You could spend more here, of course. On the à la carte menus, luncheon entrées go up to $25 for veal chop Tchoupitoulas, and dinner entrées top out at $37 for prime sirloin strip. But these prices, too, are fair, given the quality of the ingredients, the care that goes into their preparation, and the level of service.

Something else that keeps the cost of your meal under control is the wide range of wines by the glass. There are always six to ten each of reds and whites, priced from $5 to $8 per glass, plus champagne at $8 to $10 per glass.

Running your eye down the list of entrées, you realize that deciding on one will not be easy. At lunch, you might want something light, such as a sandwich of marinated, grilled, and roasted vegetables on house-made onion bread, with herb goat cheese and vegetable chips. On the hearty side is a mixed grill that includes a medallion of beef, wild mushroom sausage, homemade andouille sausage, and grilled pork tenderloin, accompanied by black-eyed-pea ragout and a salad of tat soi and pea sprouts.

For dinner, will it be the Lyonnaise Gulf fish, or perhaps the daily special: sea-salt-encrusted Gulf fish served over a ragout of Georgia sweet corn,

Sweet Cause For Alarm

Meals at Commander's, always served with a flair, are sometimes finished with a flare. Most renowned, perhaps, is bananas Foster, the spectacular dessert created at Brennan's on Royal Street in the 1950s and named for one Dick Foster. A friend of Owen E. Brennan, Sr., Foster served on the Vice Committee in the French Quarter as (you might have guessed) vice-chairman. The dessert that commemorates him is prepared at tableside and begins with bananas sautéed in butter with brown sugar and cinnamon. Banana liqueur and rum are added and flambéed. When the flames die out, the mixture is poured over vanilla ice cream.

At Commander's you can also have a flamed coffee, café brûlot. Coffee, brandy, Triple Sec, and cinnamon sticks are heated together in a special brûlot bowl. The brandy is ignited, and the mixture is stirred with a ladle that is lifted high, raising the flaming liquid. Then, the brûlot master, still wielding the ladle, holds a fork with clove-studded spirals of orange peel and lemon peel in his other hand and ladles the mixture over them. (The dramatic flaming spirals that shoot forth once flamed high enough to set off the restaurant's fire alarm.) Coffee is added slowly—and carefully—until the flames die out and the café brûlot is ready to serve.

In the Coliseum Room, the striking mural features handpainted irises, foxgloves, and a Japanese holly.

For the indecisive, there is Soups 1-1-1: a cupful each of turtle soup *au sherry* and two others.

jalapeño, and bell peppers and finished with a thyme compound butter and Louisiana crawfish tails? Then there is the roasted Mississippi quail, boned and filled with Creole crawfish sausage, served with sautéed corn and jalapeño and a touch of port and quail glaze reduction; or the Colorado roast rack of lamb with a Creole mustard crust and muscadine lamb sauce served with a bouquet of vegetables, or. . . The temptations seem endless.

At one point there is help for the indecisive diner. Commander's has long been known for the appetizer Soups 1-1-1: a demitasse cupful each of the famed turtle soup *au sherry*, gumbo du jour, and soup du jour.

As the menu says, the jazz brunch is a celebration, and the fare is especially festive. It begins with a Commander's Palace Bloody Mary seasoned with horseradish, house-made Worcestershire sauce, Commander's pepper sauce, and a vegetable juice blend. It is garnished with pickled vegetables and topped off with frozen vodka poured at your table. Next comes Egg Sardou: poached egg on creamed spinach and a fresh artichoke bottom, topped with Hollandaise sauce. The dish was created in 1908 at Antoine's, another landmark New Orleans restaurant. That is followed by roasted Mississippi quail. Dessert? Creole bread pudding soufflé, its whiskey sauce, like the frozen vodka, added at your table.

The service is an efficient team effort, the waitstaff solicitous but not obtrusive. They "read the table" to determine what is appropriate, and then they quietly provide it. When one of them asks, "How's y'all's desserts?" you know that your response matters. As operations manager Steve Woodruff says, "When the servers see the smile on the customer's face, the wow!, that energizes them."

Now it is time for that after-dinner drink at the bar.

Commander's recognizes potential:
Hired as a temporary busboy,
Richard Shakespeare is now general
manager.

Commander's Palace

CHAPTER SEVEN

A TEAM WITH STAYING POWER

Operations manager Steve Woodruff did *not* want to work at Commander's Palace. The Brennans pursued him for six months before they persuaded him to join them. He has never regretted the decision.

For executive chef Jamie Shannon, barely aware of Creole cooking when he came to the restaurant in the 1980s, Commander's has provided the impetus for a new cuisine and the basis for a worldwide reputation.

Richard Shakespeare was undecided about a career when he took an interim job as a busboy at Commander's Palace in the 1970s. He rose through the ranks to become general manager and is a key person in the organization.

Dining room manager Oscar Hernandez, unlike Woodruff, was so eager to work at Commander's that in 1989 he took a job there that represented a significant demotion for him.

Maître d' George Rico has been on the scene since the 1960s. Ella Brennan fired him many times in the early years, but she always hired him back.

These are typical of the people who make Commander's Palace the special place it is, and they have different stories to tell about why they came and why they stay.

"I grew up in New Orleans," says Woodruff. "I had

this image of Commander's Palace. These were *the Brennans*, probably doing things the same way they did 20 years ago. Would they want my ideas? That was my biggest fear about coming to work here."

When Woodruff finally did agree to come aboard, the job didn't work out quite the way it was supposed to. "The purchasing agent, Miss Jill, had been with the family for 35 years," he recalls, "and she was an encyclopedia of restaurant products. The Brennans needed someone to take over when she retired, so I learned Miss Jill's job and assisted her."

There was one complication, however. The Brennans had given Miss Jill lifetime job security, and she did not retire until she was 72. As Woodruff waited in the wings for nine years, he took over other duties that prepared him for his present role. As operations manager, he is responsible for development of the noncooking management staff, including dining room managers and kitchen managers. He supervises people in sales, reservations, and maintenance and works with the culinary management on controlling costs and planning budgets.

Obviously, Woodruff's biggest fear didn't materialize. He found that the Brennans very much wanted his ideas. "Ella loves to pick people's brains," he says. "She'll say, 'Got five minutes? Come over and we'll talk.' And you emerge from her house two hours later."

He was surprised to find that his ideas counted more at Commander's than they had at the corporate restaurant where he had worked for 14 years. "There, things were dictated," he says. "Here, it's more partnering with people. We bounce things off each other, appreciate each other's opinions."

Shakespeare admits that he "fell into this business." In college, he says, "I didn't have a clear major. But I knew that I didn't want to sit at a desk all day." No danger of that in his role managing the front of the house, which includes waiters, managers, and anyone else who interacts with the customers.

At Commander's, that is a lot of people. For every six-table station, there is a team of three: a captain, a front waiter, and a back waiter.

Chef Shannon's award-winning cuisine blends Creole traditions with his own innovations.

"When we want to move to the next level, we adjust, we fine-tune till we get there."
—Steve Woodruff, operations manager

The captain "introduces himself to the table, hands out menus, takes orders, and is responsible for everything that happens on the station," says Shakespeare. The front waiter handles all beverage service but is responsible for more than just providing cocktails, wine, and coffee. "The front waiter should be able to take an order and know most of what the captain knows," says the general manager. The back waiter serves the water and bread, takes dessert orders, and buses and resets the tables.

Add to those teams the 25 runners plus the dining room managers and you get an impressive per-table ratio. "That's what we need to deliver the service," says Shakespeare. During any meal, there will be ten or more runners at work. Besides delivering trays, they help seat arriving guests and perform kitchen cleanup chores.

"The food runners are a tremendous example of a team," says Woodruff. "There's a lot of peer pressure on them to pull their weight. Everything they do is supporting someone else."

Woodruff, Shakespeare, and Shannon, the triumvirate responsible for day-to-day operations at Commander's, set the goals for the staff. And they keep raising the performance bar. Says Woodruff, "When we want to move to the next level, we adjust, we fine-tune till we get there."

In each dining room, though, it is the dining room manager who supervises the service teams and makes sure that the Brennans' standards are met. Dining room managers interview, hire, and train the teams of waiters.

Oscar Hernandez arrived at the position of dining room manager by an unusual route. When he came to Commander's seeking a job, he was comfortably employed as a maître d' at one of New Orleans' finer hotels. The only opening at Commander's was for a food runner. To some people, that entry-level post might have looked like a giant step in the wrong direction, but

Maître d' George Rico has an uncanny ability to remember patrons and their preferences.

INSIGHTS ON WINE AND LIKING MIKE

"Yesterday at dinner I noticed something that's a pet peeve of mine," operations manager Steve Woodruff is saying. "Even when there's nothing on a tray, you should carry it like a tray."

At 10:45 a.m. and 5:15 p.m. each day, Commander's Palace waiters, food runners, and dining room managers assemble for a "pre-meal." Though brief, these sessions cover a wide range of topics. On this bright, warm day, Woodruff is conducting the meeting outdoors on the Garden Patio.

"It's not a chest protector," he continues, using both hands to hold a tray against his chest. "It's not a Frisbee"; he holds the tray between his fingers and swings it. Then, balancing the empty tray on the palm of his upraised hand, he demonstrates the correct technique. He has made his point, and he quickly moves on to another topic.

For the waitstaff, the pre-meal is both a briefing on the specials they are about to serve and a short training session. Sometimes a dining room manager will review service standards or provide feedback on something that occurred during the previous meal. General manager Richard Shakespeare, who oversees the wine cellar, might offer some wine insights.

Next, Woodruff follows up on a topic dear to the heart of Ella Brennan, who sets the standards for staff performance and advises employees on living up to them. "In the captains' meeting yesterday, Ella was talking a lot about mentoring," Woodruff says. "If you have knowledge, share it. If you haven't been here for long, look for people who have. Ask questions. We see a lot of people here doing a good job, being successful. If you don't feel you're being successful, observe. Look for role models. What is that person doing?"

Just before the meeting ends, Woodruff hands out photocopies of a narrative titled, "You Gotta Like Mike." Watching TV one night, Woodruff was so taken with the story about Mike Edwards, Jr., that he summarized it for the pre-meal. Edwards was born with a deformed leg that eventually had to be amputated and replaced with a prosthesis. But he was so determined to become an athlete that he qualified for the basketball team not only in high school but also at the University of Notre Dame.

Inspired by the account, Woodruff translated it into a motivational message for his people. "At a very young age," he wrote, "Mike learned that life comes with adversity. Getting the most out of life means overcoming it. Mike is a hero, a role model, a problem solver, and so much more. YOU GOTTA LIKE MIKE!"

Most people scan the photocopied sheets. A few tuck it away for future consumption. Woodruff's final remark as the group leaves: "Let's walk out winners today!"

"It's a tray, not a Frisbee," Steve Woodruff says, as he demonstrates the correct technique.

Hernandez knew better. He saw it as a foot in the door of one of the greatest restaurants in the world, and he accepted the job. His explanation: "I like to know a place inside out."

Hernandez did not remain entry-level for long, because his qualifications and potential were apparent to the Brennans. "I was taking wine courses, and they could see that I was interested," he says. He moved up quickly through the dining room ranks.

Watching Hernandez on duty in the Parlor Room, it is obvious that he is passionate about his work. He stands at the back of the room ramrod straight, head held high, eyes in constant motion as he surveys the tables. Nothing escapes him. When a runner appears with a tray from the kitchen, he scans the plates, checking them against the order to ensure that everything is as it should be. Then he quickly assembles the service team, bringing together as many people as are needed for Commander's signature gang service.

*Ella Brennan sets the standards for
performance at Commander's.*

"I was kind of wild," admits maître d' George Rico. "Once a week, Miss Ella would fire me."

Of all the lore surrounding Commander's Palace, maître d' Rico's story borders on the epic. It dates back to 1962, when he was a newspaper delivery boy and his customers included Frank and Elinor Moran, owners of the restaurant. One day, during one of the downpours for which New Orleans is famed, Rico delivered the Morans' newspaper and then ducked under the shelter of their porch waiting for the storm to pass. Frank Moran caught sight of Rico when he came out to retrieve his newspaper and struck up a conversation. After a few minutes, he offered him a job.

No detail escapes the eye of dining room manager Oscar Hernandez.

The job? "I took the dirty dishes from the elevator to the dish room," Rico recalls. But gradually he advanced to assistant dishwasher, then busboy, then waiter. One of his customers was Adelaide Brennan.

"I used to wait on Miss Adelaide," he says. "One day, she came in with Miss Ella and they told me they had just bought the restaurant." Rico stayed on as a waiter, but it was a bumpy ride. "I was kind of wild," he admits. "Once a week, Miss Ella would fire me."

Not only did Ella Brennan always rehire him, she eventually promoted him. One day she told him to wear a suit the next day so that he could follow the maître d' around and learn his job. When the man retired, Rico was ready to take over.

Rico's knowledge of customers and their preferences makes him invaluable to the organization. "I have an incredible memory for connecting names with faces," he says. "There's always something you remember—the eyes, the ears, the hair."

He also appreciates the opportunity he has been given. "The Brennans taught me a lot," he says. "I hate to think what my life would have been without their influence."

For her part, Ella does not hesitate to praise her former nemesis. Rico, she proclaims matter-of-factly, is "the most important maître d' in town."

*People who come to work at Commander's
find that they have entered a
legendary culinary training ground.*

AN EXTENDED FAMILY THAT LETS YOU GROW

*F*requent staff turnover is common in the restaurant industry. Why do people stay at Commander's Palace for years, even decades? Two reasons are apparent: the opportunity to learn from the best, and the opportunity to grow and advance.

"A lot of people come here to get Commander's Palace on their résumé," says operations manager Steve Woodruff. "They plan to stay for a year, but that year passes and they say, 'Wow! Look what I've learned, and what's still ahead of me.' So they stay." They find that they can move up through the ranks, taking on more and more responsibilities.

But there is something else that keeps people at Commander's: the satisfaction of working for owners who are considerate of their employees. "I get offers to work at other places," says maître d' George Rico. "But the Brennans take care of you, they're nice to you, they worry about you and your family. They *feel* like family."

Rico's opinion is shared by just about everyone who works at the restaurant, and that has a profound impact on the organization. Says Richard Shakespeare, "The Brennans are always good about giving you two days off in a row, two days that are yours so you can have a personal life. Not many restaurants do that."

These people speak fondly of jobs they keep because they enjoy them, jobs that are rewarding and satisfying. Their satisfaction is reflected in the way they treat their coworkers and their patrons. As a result, sincere customer care is woven into the fabric of the organization.

Commander's is an elegant-but-unstuffy restaurant where patrons know they can relax.

Commander's Palace

CHAPTER EIGHT

WHERE CELEBRITIES CAN FEEL AT HOME

It was a Saturday, always a busy day at Commander's Palace. But this was "one of the busiest Saturdays," recalls George Rico. There was a geologists' convention in town, and Commander's is a favorite of conventioneers.

The maître d' was busily greeting the arriving patrons when a young man came in and asked for a table for five. He had no reservation. Impossible? Not necessarily. He showed Rico his Secret Service identification and explained that former President Ronald Reagan had just given a speech in town and wanted to have lunch at Commander's. When would Reagan arrive? Rico asked. The reply: He was at that moment outside in a limousine.

Rico worked his managerial magic. "I told the staff to get a corner table ready fast," he says. When Reagan came into the restaurant, he was so grateful that "he gave me two hugs," says Rico. "And on his way out, he said 'Thank you' in Spanish." Rico is from Honduras and retains his Latin accent. He was touched by Reagan's awareness and sensitivity.

Being personally acknowledged by a former President of the United States makes a great story, of course, but it's just one of many about the VIPs who come to Commander's Palace. Celebrities initially choose the restaurant for the same reasons that everyone else does, for its outstanding food, faultless service, unpretentious elegance, and a fun time. But Commander's offers prominent people something else that they value highly: privacy.

"When movie stars or big names come in, we don't let anybody bother them," says Rico. When actor Woody Allen was dining at Commander's with Soon-Yi Previn, before the couple was married, he

Although Bruce Springsteen likes to have brunch in the Garden Room, you won't spot him in this picture.

says, "A woman gave me a camera and said she'd give me a thousand dollars if I took a picture of them kissing or holding hands. I said I don't do that."

Occasionally the staff is pressed into service to provide an extra measure of privacy. When newscaster Walter Cronkite came to dinner, says general manager Richard Shakespeare, "A manager and I had to stand on either side of him to keep people away while he ate."

There was one occasion when the security was breached, however. "Bruce Springsteen likes to come here for brunch, and he was in the Garden Room," says Shakespeare. "It was a high school ring day, and there were many teenage girls here. We had to tell them they couldn't go into the Garden Room." The room, of course, has a huge window wall overlooking the lush Garden Patio. When an older woman, definitely not a teenager, came into the room to take a photograph of the Patio, no one tried to stop her, because she didn't fit the profile. But then she whirled around and snapped her Springsteen shot. Too late; the deed was done.

Although the managers go out of their way to protect the privacy of celebrity patrons, the rest of the staff really doesn't do anything differently for them, says Shakespeare. "Commander's Palace is used to having high-profile people here. In the main dining room and the Garden Room especially, they're used to it. They just go about their normal routine."

So the celebrities keep coming. There was the time that Margaret Thatcher was there. "I got to meet the head of Scotland Yard," says Shakespeare. "That's more impressive than meeting actors."

Just two days before that, there had been an even more impressive show of strength. John Major, another former prime minister of Britain, was in the restaurant at the same time as

A Private Entrance
For the Locals

It is not just lip service when Commander's Palace calls itself a local restaurant, and the locals know it. Told that a book was being written about the New Orleans landmark, taxi driver Dolores Nenera says emphatically, "Well, you can put this in the book: They take care of the locals. If you tell them you're a local, you'll get in."

How can that be done? How does the restaurant hold back enough tables without making the mistake of holding back too many?

"It's like a chess game," Lally Brennan says, "knowing how your house works. You have no-shows, people who eat faster than others, people coming out to have fun and staying a little longer." It takes enormous attention to detail and a keen insight into people to make it all work.

To encourage the locals even more, Commander's launched its Back Door Campaign. Certain local people, "the foodies, the movers and shakers," says Lally, are given a working key to the door that leads from the bar onto the Garden Patio. Each of the managers takes five keys and hands them out to people they think should have them. Keys have been given, for example, to Paul McIlheny, head of the company that makes Tabasco sauce, and to the president of one of the local banks.

Anyone who has a key can come in through the back door, walk up to the bar, phone the maître d' and say he'd like a table now; no reservation is necessary. The keys are symbolic, of course, since the back door is always unlocked when the restaurant is open. But they are a way to make people feel special and encourage them to come to Commander's more often.

"Ella likes to pick people's brains," says operations manager Steve Woodruff.

"Truman Capote was in town, so I asked him if he'd come to dinner. I wanted to give him to Adelaide for her birthday."—*Dottie Brennan-Bridgeman*

"It's up to the staff to know, and provide, whatever the regular customers want," says general manager Richard Shakespeare.

the chief executive of a leading U.S. computer company. "We had British and U.S. security here," says Shakespeare. "That's the most security I've ever seen, except for when the bishop of Nicaragua was here." There had been unrest in Nicaragua at that time and it was feared that there might be an attempt on the bishop's life while he was out of his country.

Perhaps because it gives them a chance to be elegantly casual, Commander's has always been popular with show people. "If there's a movie star in town, they come here," says Dottie Brennan-Bridgeman, as do theater and TV personalities.

Actor Raymond Burr was a regular, not just a patron but "one of Miss Ella's best friends," says Rico. Several people on the staff at Commander's talk about the time, not long before Burr's death, that he was in New Orleans for three days and dined at Commander's each day. Just before he left the city, says Rico, "he sent Miss Ella so many flowers they wouldn't fit into the house, so we put them in the restaurant."

New Orleans has attracted and nurtured many writers. Anne Rice, for example, made a distinct impression on operations manager Steve Woodruff. "One night, on the *Tonight* show," says Woodruff, "she said, 'When I die, I want to be buried in Lafayette Cemetery, across

JUST WHAT THE DOCTOR ORDERED—AND THEN SOME

How far will the Commander's Palace staff go to grant a customer's wish? Here is a story that answers the question in no uncertain terms.

A visitor from out of state had been eagerly anticipating dinner at Commander's when—bad luck!—she fell ill. She ended up in the hospital and had to cancel her reservation. So distraught was she about missing dinner that she mentioned it to the intern who admitted her to the hospital. Apparently the illness imposed no restrictions on the woman's diet, because the intern had the bright idea of calling Commander's and asking if it was possible to order bread pudding soufflé to go. Chef Jamie Shannon was able to do better than that. He put together an entire meal of shrimp, filet mignon, and, of course, the bread pudding soufflé. He plated it on the restaurant's signature dinnerware and sent it over to the hospital, compliments of Commander's, so that the patient didn't miss her dinner after all.

That would be a great story even if it ended there, but it doesn't. It turns out that most people at Commander's didn't know anything about the incident until they read an item in a local newspaper. The intern was so impressed by the exceptional service that he called the newspaper, but Shannon and his crew never said anything to anyone. To them, extraordinary service is standard operating procedure. If a customer, even a would-be customer, wants something, Commander's staff finds a way to provide it.

*The focus is on local,
seasonal produce.*

"When movie stars or big names come in, we don't let anybody bother them."

—George Rico, maître d'

the street from my favorite restaurant, Commander's Palace.'" Rice's family does, in fact, have a plot in the landmark cemetery.

"Back in the old days," says Dottie, "our customers included Leon Uris, Robert Ruark, and Lillian Hellman. Tennessee Williams came here on Sunday nights." Dottie is all cool, stylish elegance, but her mischievous side occasionally shows through. "Truman Capote was here. He was in town, holed up writing, and he came in for breakfast. I asked him if he would come to dinner. I wanted to give him to Adelaide for her birthday."

A little more mischief. "Sean Connery came in one day," says Dottie. "Here was this short, bald man. If it weren't for his voice, we wouldn't have recognized him."

The list goes on: the Emperor of Japan, Henry Kissinger, Princess Margaret, Ann-Margret, Steve McQueen, Edward G. Robinson, Jerry Seinfeld, Bob Hope, Carol Burnett, Phyllis Diller. But you will never know about any of the famous guests unless you ask. There isn't a single photograph of a celebrity to be seen in the restaurant. That, too, would be an invasion of the guests' privacy.

The lack of celebrity photographs dovetails with the Brennans' style. They don't tire of telling you how hard they work to make their restaurant the best, but at the same time, they remain modest, even self-effacing. It would never occur to them to brag about rubbing shoulders with the rich, the famous, and the powerful.

"I admit that meeting these people is an exciting part of the business," says Ella. "But the people you fall in love with are the everyday people."

Patrons fortunate enough to dine at the chef's table can visit with chef Shannon. Opposite page, the variety on Commander's menu makes choosing a challenge.

What better way to celebrate New Year's Eve than with Commander's Palace's private label California champagne.

Commander's Palace

CHAPTER NINE

GOOD TIMES AT A GREAT RESTAURANT

Ask Brad Brennan if he recalls any special days at Commander's Palace and he pauses for a moment, a mischievous look crosses his face, and he asks, "Good or bad?"

If he seems amused by the question, it is because two occasions pop into his mind. The best night by far came in 1996, when Commander's won the James Beard Award for Outstanding Restaurant in the United States. The worst was a year earlier, when the restaurant *didn't* win the award, although that setback turned out to be the least disastrous part of the evening.

"Lally and I were in town," Brad recalls. "Ella, Ti, Dick, and Dickie were in New York City for the ceremony." Everyone connected with Commander's was crushed, of course, when word came that they hadn't won the award. But even the gods looking down on New Orleans must have wept, because it rained, and rained, and rained. The Brennans' disappointment was about to be compounded by disaster.

"I got in the next morning about 5 a.m. to help with the inventory," Brad continues. "I knew we had some

Even in the face of natural disaster, says Brad Brennan, "We don't stop. We just keep going."

flooding, but I didn't know the extent of the damage." Heading toward the kitchen, he walked past pots, pans, and dishes stacked on the floor. When he reached the kitchen, "I saw Lally, Steve Woodruff, and a couple of our other people sitting at the chef's table, looking shocked. There was a foot of water in the restaurant, maybe two feet on the patio."

What were they to do? How could they clean up the mess and get the restaurant up and running by evening? Brad sprang into action. "I had a truck that could go through the water, so I rounded up our best kitchen managers to get us squared away. I called them and said, 'If you don't have a way to get here, stand outside your house and I'll pick you up.'" Everyone pitched in and by that evening, the second floor of the restaurant was open for dinner. "We don't stop," Brad says matter-of-factly. "We just keep going."

The following year, things turned out a little better. Commander's Palace prevailed in the James Beard stakes, and Lally and Dickie Brennan and Jamie Shannon were in New York to accept the award. When they called to tell the people at Commander's that they had won, says Brad, "Ella ran into each dining room in the restaurant, clanging a fork against a glass and crying out, 'We won! We just won the James Beard Award! You all are eating in the best restaurant in the country!'"

For most people at Commander's, the day they won the "Outstanding" award is the outstanding moment in the restaurant's history. But apart from that, some of the

Brad Brennan waded in to help after Commander's great flood—at no small risk to his treasured chili pepper socks.

A Vote for Commander's Palace

Commander's Palace is a favorite of politicians, national as well as local. It was a favorite gathering spot in 1988, for instance, when the Republican National Convention was held in New Orleans and George Bush was nominated as the candidate for president. Dottie Brennan-Bridgeman recalls that one evening, before Bush had chosen his running mate, "Ella was walking through the dining room and she kept hearing people talk about 'Quayle.' She wondered, was everyone ordering the quail? Or was something wrong with it?" Little did Ella realize that she was overhearing ruminations of Dan Quayle's selection as the vice-presidential candidate.

It was also during that convention, says Dottie, that the media flocked to Commander's after an event at the convention center. "I was having dinner with Art Buchwald, and he said to me, 'You have every national media person in the country here. What are you going to do about it?'"

The Brennans have always had good promotional sense. Remember that they persuaded the Travel Holiday Awards organizers to bring the awards ceremony to New Orleans as a way to publicize the city, and they invited the American Cuisine Symposium to meet in New Orleans and have dinner at Commander's. But the media were already in New Orleans, already at Commander's. What else could the Brennans do?

Ella's solution was simple, says Dottie: "She invited them all to our house for champagne." The invitees included Tom Brokaw, David Brinkley, Peter Jennings, Cokie Roberts, Sam Donaldson, George Will, and Sander Vanocur. It was an influential group enjoying a special evening.

Centuries-old live oak trees shade the Garden Patio.

A PRICELESS OPINION

Milton Friedman, the Nobel Prize-winning economist, was having dinner at Commander's Palace one evening with his wife and two professors from Tulane University. Ti Martin stopped by to chat with the group. "I was thrilled to have Mr. Friedman in the restaurant," she says, partly because of his stature but also because she had been taught by his son, David, a professor at Tulane, when she was studying for her MBA.

With the conversation ranging from dinner to economics, it was no surprise that someone asked Ti how the restaurant was doing. When she replied that business was strong, one of the professors remarked, "At Commander's prices, I guess things are good." Ti had a response ready—*Food & Wine* magazine had just named Commander's Palace the best value in New Orleans—but she didn't get a chance to use it. Friedman got there first. Noting the full dining room, he said, "I'd say they've got the prices figured just right."

most memorable days have been the celebrations and traditions that the managers have launched themselves. The Brennans have a highly developed sense of style, a talent for promoting their business, and they love to have a good time.

St. Patrick's Day, for example, is a day of great significance for people named Brennan, and it was especially festive in the early years of the restaurant. "Dick and John would invite their best customers to a party in the Patio Room," Richard Shakespeare recalls. "There's a pub nearby called Parasols that has a block party. It's the center of the Irish celebration—probably 10,000 people attend. People would come here for our St. Patrick's Day party, then walk over to Parasols for the block party."

Nowadays, Commander's is the stepping-off point for another renowned parade, this one on Mardi Gras. Clarinetist Pete Fountain and his marching band start their day with sandwiches at Commander's. Thus fortified, they march from the Garden District to the French Quarter to join the city's official celebration.

But just because the band has departed doesn't mean the party is over at Commander's. Once guests walk through the balloon-and-ribbon-filled foyer, they find the entire restaurant looking festive. There are paper crowns on each table so that everyone can be a Mardi Gras king or queen. And there is traditional New Orleans "second line" dancing: people do a line-dance through the restaurant waving their table napkins above their heads.

Come autumn, Commander's plays an important role in New Orleans during the holiday season. "Ten

*Commander's started the
New Orleans tradition of giving guests
Christmas bells.*

Before stepping off in the Mardi Gras parade, Pete Fountain and his marching band start their day with sandwiches at Commander's.

Many of the floats (above and right) for the famed Mardi Gras parade are constructed at Blaine Kern's Mardi Gras World.

years ago, the idea of having Thanksgiving dinner in a restaurant seemed wrong to me," says Steve Woodruff, observing that he, like many other family men, has changed his mind. "Now I feel I want to be with my family, enjoy them, and not have all that work. I come here in the morning, work till three, and sometimes have my family meet me here."

Many New Orleanians share his desire to enjoy a drudgery-free Thanksgiving Day with their families. "It's a very busy day," Woodruff says. "We open at 11:30 in the morning and serve continuously until 8 p.m. A lot of our regular customers come. We'll have large parties, 10 or 12 people; there can be three generations at the same table." For those families, a "traditional" Thanksgiving means having dinner at Commander's.

Although Commander's closes on Christmas Eve and Christmas Day, there are celebrations throughout the preceding two weeks. Carolers stroll from room to room, filling the air with holiday melodies. During those two weeks, every customer who walks in is given a jingle bell on a ribbon to wear around his neck. Says Woodruff, "We started it, and now all the restaurants do it." (Chalk up another first for Commander's.) A couple of years ago, he adds, "one of our regular customers had two Christmas trees at home. One was traditional, and one was decorated with the bells he's collected from all the restaurants."

PARTY TIME!

Celebrations reach their peak on New Year's Eve. "It's like a private party," says Woodruff. "Most of the people here are regulars who come year after year. We seat people at 8 o'clock and they stay for the evening. We don't turn the tables. The menu is upgraded, but the prices are not as high as in other restaurants."

There is a band in each dining room for the entire evening,

A perfect ending: Dining room manager Ray Brinkman fires up a serving of the ever-popular bananas Foster.

New Year's Eve revelers covet these confetti-filled champagne poppers.

and people rearrange the tables to create dance floors. The front window-wall of the Patio Dining Room is piled high with balloons, and in every dining room there are tiaras, party hats, party favors, and noisemakers. Most coveted of all are the champagne poppers. Pull the string hanging from the mouth of these mini champagne bottles, there's a popping sound, and confetti comes flying out. Lally Brennan says she has seen guests, whom she presumed to be adults, hoarding the champagne poppers beneath the table so they could keep getting more. No wonder that, as Woodruff says, "At the end of the evening, it's a confetti nightmare."

Not that the "nightmare" ends when the evening does. When you're back at home, says Lally, and you lean over the bathroom sink to brush your teeth, confetti tumbles from your hair. The next time you try to put on your dress shoes, they feel too tight, and you realize that it's because the toes are crammed with the stuff.

After a night like that, you'd think Commander's management and the staff would like a day off to recover. Not a chance. "On January 1, the Sugar Bowl game is in town and we do a jazz brunch," says Woodruff. "It takes some pretty good determination to do New Year's Eve, get the place clean, and then do New Year's Day."

Determination, yes, but as Brad Brennan observed, Commander's is a place that never pauses. Why would they want to stop when they, and their guests, are having so much fun?

Commander's bright shining moment: Jamie Shannon, Lally Brennan, and Dickie Brennan accept the James Beard Foundation's award for Outstanding Restaurant in the United States.

Commander's Palace

CHAPTER TEN

A FAVORITE OF HAUT MONDE AND HOI POLLOI ALIKE

Ever since the Brennan family has managed Commander's Palace, it has consistently won the praise of food writers and reaped countless awards for the quality of its food and service. Perhaps the most memorable moment came in 1996 when the restaurant won the James Beard Foundation's Outstanding Restaurant Award, a goal that had long been at the top of the Brennans' list.

Indeed, 1996 was a blockbuster year for Commander's. In addition to being honored by the James Beard Foundation, it got a promotional lift when *New Orleans* magazine named Jamie Shannon Chef of the Year. Then, readers of *Southern Living* magazine chose Commander's as their favorite city restaurant—which they've done every year since. It was also the first year that a *Zagat Survey* was published for New Orleans, and Commander's ranked as the most popular restaurant in the city, a distinction it has retained in each subsequent survey.

There have been other big years since then. In 1998 Shannon was cited again by *New Orleans* magazine as the best chef in town, and *Food and Wine* magazine gave Commander's two honors, naming it the "quintessential New Orleans restaurant" and the best value in New Orleans. In addition, *Wine Spectator* presented Commander's

The awards range widely because
Commander's aims to be many things to many
people—and it succeeds.

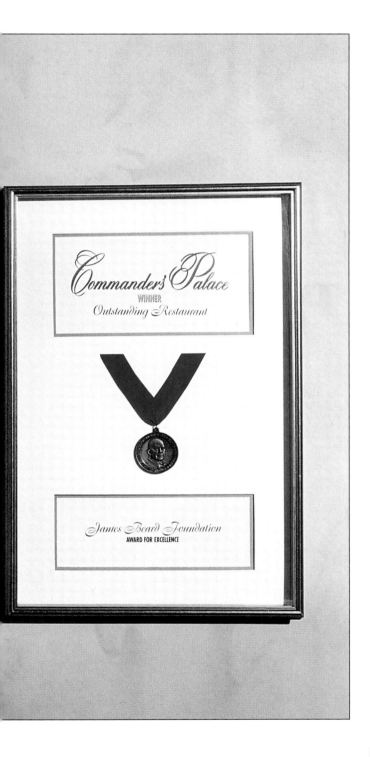

with an Award of Excellence for its wine list.

There seems to be no end to the accolades. They come from sources as diverse as *The Robb Report for the Luxury Lifestyle* and *Rolling Stone;* from judges ranging from the culinary elite to foodies to people who simply know what they like.

The awards range widely because Commander's aims to be many things to many people—and it succeeds. It is an unpretentious place where you can relax and be yourself; yet it is an ideal spot for a special occasion. Tourists flock there, but it remains a local favorite. It is a top choice for business entertaining, yet it works well for marriage proposals, too. Shannon wins awards for his contemporary cuisine; but the menu is never intimidating and the food never looks fussy.

Rick Bragg, writing in *The New York Times,* makes the point precisely. Calling Commander's "the best restaurant in the city," he observes that although "snobs say it is too touristy now . . . that is bald pretension." Bragg's advice: Eat the bread pudding soufflé. And he makes that sound like both an admonishment to the snobs and a recommendation to everyone else. *Rolling Stone,* hardly an elitist magazine, has called Commander's "the spiritual home of contemporary New Orleans cooking."

Looking for a down-to-earth review? Check out this one from *GambitWeekly,* a local publication: "In case you've forgotten (yeah, right), Commander's Palace rules the New Orleans restaurant scene. The ven-

The three James Beard Foundation awards, for Outstanding Service in the United States, Best Chef in the Southeast, and Outstanding Restaurant in the United States.

OFTEN FULL BUT NEVER CROWDED

*T*he best reviews of Commander's Palace offer insights into the personality of the restaurant and reveal the large degree to which the Brennan managers have achieved their goals for cuisine and service. For example, the restaurant index at Fodor's Travel Online, the Web site maintained by the guidebook publisher, states that "no restaurant captures New Orleans's gastronomic heritage and celebratory spirit as well as this one in a stately Garden District mansion. . . . Several hundred people might dine at Commander's on a given day, but its size rarely interferes with the quality of the food or service."

Also impressed with Commander's ability to maintain high quality on a large scale is Eric Asimov, a food critic for *The New York Times*. "Old fashioned Creole cooking . . . is offered at Commander's with consummate grace and ease," Asimov wrote in an article titled "New Orleans, a City of Serious Eaters." He also remarked that "it's all the more noteworthy because Commander's is such a huge operation, serving an astonishing volume of food seamlessly and beautifully."

It isn't just the efficiency of the service that Asimov appreciates, of course; he also has high praise for the food: "The turtle soup here, with lots of pepper and bits of turtle, has spirit and depth, made with a stock that doesn't just deliver flavor but soars high before easing into a long finish." After feasting on Commander's crawfish maque choux and the roasted boned quail, Asimov stated, "Our main courses were uniformly wonderful." As for dessert, the strawberry shortcake is "the perfect end to a rich meal. If you're after something more solid, though, you couldn't do better than the cheesecake made with Creole cream cheese."

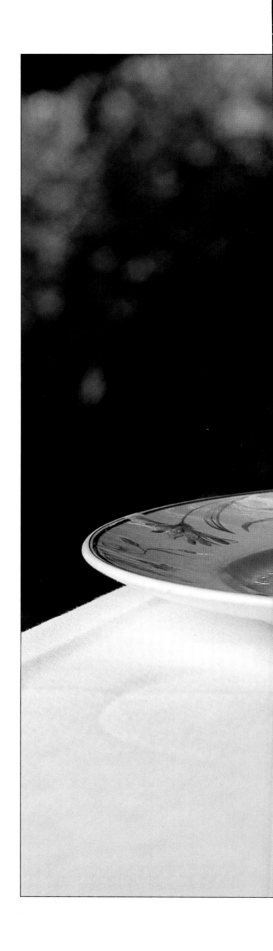

The famed Creole cream cheese cake, topped with a chocolate and white chocolate lattice.

"Commander's Palace is clearly a culinary mecca, whether you live in New Orleans or not."

—Food and Wine *magazine*

TAKING THE BEARD AWARDS
IN STRIDE

A photo taken at the James Beard Foundation awards ceremony in 1996 shows Lally Brennan standing at a podium, right hand over her heart. "I look as though I'm saying the Pledge of Allegiance," she says with a laugh. She explains that, in truth, her heart was pounding so hard she was afraid it would burst from her chest.

Why? Because this was the third consecutive year in which Commander's Palace had been nominated for the foundation's Outstanding Restaurant designation. There are only five nominees nationwide, which means that just being nominated is an achievement. Twice before, Commander's had been shut out. Sitting in the audience, Lally was concentrating so hard on rehearsing the acceptance speech she had prepared that she didn't hear Commander's name announced as the winner. Dickie Brennan and Jamie Shannon, who were sitting with her, had to rouse her. Then the three walked to the podium to accept the award.

Back in New Orleans, Ella Brennan was elated. The goal she had set during Commander's early years had at last been reached. No wonder she ran through the restaurant shouting that Commander's Palace had been named the best restaurant in the country.

Commander's has had its share of other James Beard awards as well. In 1999, Shannon was named Best Chef in the Southeast, and in 1993 Ella had her own shining moment when Commander's won the award for outstanding service. Richard Shakespeare, Commander's service guru, escorted Ella to the stage. When the award was handed to her, she turned it over to Shakespeare, then delivered an acceptance speech that was both brief and gracious: "I receive this for all the waiters and captains in the whole damn country!"

Skilled chefs and cooks are on chef Shannon's team.

erable institution remains as vital as ever, especially with executive chef Jamie Shannon running the kitchen. It is the crown jewel of the Brennan legacy."

Commander's has also received favorable notices from its peers and from industry publications. It won its first Award of Excellence from the Distinguished Restaurants of North America (DiRōNa) in 1993 and has remained on the list ever since. A restaurant qualifies for the award by passing a 75-point evaluation conducted anonymously by industry professionals, and retains the award for three years if it continues to meet all the criteria. If it passes re-inspection, it receives the award for another three-year period. Fewer than 700 restaurants in the United States, Canada, and Mexico have the DiRōNa designation.

In 1995, *Food and Wine* magazine named Commander's the top restaurant in the United States, noting that, in its annual poll, readers had mentioned Commander's three times as often as any other restaurant. According to the citation, "Commander's Palace in New Orleans is clearly a culinary mecca for many of you, whether you live in New Orleans or not."

Wine Spectator that same year asked restaurant reviewers and food writers in 14 cities to name their personal favorites. "Nowhere in America is it more important to eat the food of the region than it is in New Orleans," wrote critic Tom Fitzmorris. Consequently, "Like most Orleanians, I keep Commander's Palace on my A-list." He went on to explain that Commander's is able to do more than showcase regional cuisine. "The 115-year-old flagship of the Brennan family empire is strong both in traditional Creole dishes and in the innovative haute Creole cuisine that it helped to create."

Fitzmorris was among the first to recognize Commander's as an entity on the world culinary scene. In a 1996 article for

Ella Brennan, the queen of Commander's Palace.

*The Coliseum Room is a jewel,
with its sunny yellow walls and
sparkling chandeliers.*

"For my last meal, this is where I'd want to go."

—Tom Fitzmorris, restaurant critic

Travel & Leisure titled "Critic's Picks: World's Top Restaurants," he wrote, "For my last meal, this is where I'd want to go." Three years later, the *Robb Report for the Luxury Lifestyle,* in its 11th annual Best of the Best issue, declared Shannon the No. 2 chef not in New Orleans, not in the United States, but in the entire world.

One of the first industry magazines to single out Commander's for its quality was *Nation's Restaurant News,* which named the restaurant to its Fine Dining Hall of Fame in 1982. Another early citation came from *Sales & Marketing Management,* which polls readers annually for its Business Executives' Dining Awards (the main distinction: restaurants considered best for dining with customers and prospects). In 1986, Commander's was No.1 in the country. The popularity with businesspeople has been sustained. In 1999, readers of *Gourmet* voted Commander's Tops for Business in New Orleans.

Because it has always been popular with local diners, Commander's high scores in the *Zagat Survey* aren't surprising. Zagat prides itself on presenting the opinions of people who "are a very diverse group in every respect but one—they are food lovers all." That is clear from the kind of praise the locals have heaped on Commander's in the *Zagat Survey.* Some typical quotes: "The pinnacle of Creole food" . . . "a rarely matched experience". . . "beautiful rooms". . . "incredible service". . . "best jazz brunch in town."

Zagat's ratings are on a scale of 0 to 30, and Commander's has consistently scored in the 26-30 range, "Extraordinary to Perfection." An impressive performance. Yet you can easily imagine everyone at Commander's brainstorming, trying to come up with still more extraordinary ideas to boost the numbers even higher.

Chef Jamie Shannon, always willing to support a good cause, is one of the prime forces behind Taste of the Nation.

Commander's Palace

CHAPTER ELEVEN

LIVING UP TO A TRADITION OF GIVING

Since 1988, Share Our Strength, an antihunger and antipoverty organization, has held an annual fundraising culinary event called Taste of the Nation. In cities across the country, chefs of premier restaurants prepare their finest dishes, donating both their time and the ingredients. Tickets to the tastings are sold to the public, and every penny of the proceeds is distributed according to the following formula: 70 percent goes to food banks and other local programs, 10 percent goes to communities in the state that don't have restaurants capable of holding such an event, and 20 percent goes to needy people overseas.

In each participating city, one chef organizes the event, urging chefs at other restaurants to aid the cause. For this event, the chefs are colleagues, not competitors. "The chefs cook at the benefit, but even more important, they organize it," says Bill Shore, executive director of Share Our Strength. "We count on them to make it happen." In New Orleans, the chef who makes it happen is Jamie Shannon of Commander's Palace. In fact, Commander's chefs have participated in the benefit from the beginning.

Shannon, naturally, has the support of everyone at Commander's. "Jamie couldn't be involved if the Brennans

Ella Brennan on the era she has witnessed: "This was the beginning of America becoming a great food country."

weren't behind it," says Kimberly Penharlow, southern regional manager for Share Our Strength. "They've given us their chef, food, prep time, and dedication."

Organizers of industry and charitable events know that having the Brennans participate helps to ensure the success of any occasion. "When we have a program, the first restaurant we want to sign up is Commander's Palace," says Jim Funk, chief executive officer of the Louisiana Restaurant Association. "If it's good enough for them, it's good enough for the others."

Funk once referred to the Brennan family as "the Kennedys of New Orleans." Asked what prompted that remark, he says there were two reasons. "First, they're a close-knit family. Some have begun going out on their own, making their own mark, but people are still close." The second reason, he says, is that "the Brennan name is powerful in New Orleans, in Louisiana, and even nationally. The powerful name draws people to the restaurant."

The first generation of Commander's Palace Brennans, known locally as "the aunts and uncles," has long set the standards, not just for fine dining, but for generosity and for leadership in their industry and in their community. They are passing those standards down to "the cousins," the next generation. Ask Lally Brennan why she's involved in a long list of activities and causes, from the Audubon Zoo to the Children's Hospital, from Meals on Wheels to landmarks preservation. She replies, "We've been raised to give back to the community as much as we can."

So they have. "I give a lot of credit to Dick and Ella as the family leaders," says Funk. "Dick is a lot quieter and likes to work behind the scenes. Ella has a charismatic personality. People flock to her. She's a great trainer, a great teacher. So many people who used to work for her are successful because of what they learned from her."

Soft shell crabs will likely be on the menu when Commander's Palace hosts a charitable event.

PROUD TO CALL NEW ORLEANS HOME

*H*ow do the managers of a world-famous restaurant choose which charities and industry organizations to support? "You have a friend who gets you by the elbow, and . . . ," says Ti Martin. Her involvement ranges from the Louisiana Human Rights Campaign to the International Association of Culinary Professionals. She is also active in the New Orleans Metropolitan Convention and Visitors Bureau, the group her uncle, Dick Brennan, supported in the days when the Brennans first managed Commander's Palace. But she says she's proudest of the "New Orleans—Proud to Call It Home" campaign, which she launched in the early 1990s and then co-chaired.

"New Orleans was too dependent on the oil industry at that time," she recalls. "We were in trouble; we had the same problems every city had. We wanted to do something to improve the self-image of area residents, but we didn't want to do mindless boosterism."

To help residents focus on what was positive about their city, she says, "We did the big, obvious public relations things, TV, for example. But we always included information. We did events at the Saints games, we ran an essay contest, and the city musicians did a 'We Love New Orleans' video. We mentioned ways in which New Orleans was Number One." That *must* have included food.

Surprisingly, what caught people's imagination was the bumper sticker proclaiming "New Orleans—Proud to Call It Home." Says Ti, "The bumper stickers were a tiny part of the campaign, but that's what took off." Another idea from Commander's Palace that worked well.

Brennan cousins join forces in serving the community. Shown here, Brad Brennan, Ti Martin, Ralph Brennan, Dickie Brennan, and Lauren Brennan Brower.

"The Brennan name is powerful in New Orleans,
in Louisiana, and even nationally."

—*Jim Funk, chief executive officer of the Louisiana Restaurant Association*

A Lasting Tribute
To Ella Brennan

In recognition of her significant contribution to the industry, the New Orleans chapter of the American Culinary Federation, a 70-year-old association of chefs and cooks, in 1998 established the Ella Brennan Savoir Faire Award. The award recognizes that "Ms. Brennan, of the famed Commander's Palace restaurant, has exemplified excellence in the restaurant and hospitality industries. . . . Her talent for teaching and coaching young people with a passion for the restaurant business has led to a legion of chefs who name her as their mentor."

Ella received the award the first year. Because she was traveling at the time of the presentation, her daughter, Ti Martin, accepted for her. Ti noted that Ella has "given her heart and soul to the restaurant business and spent 50 years inspiring young people that [this] is a profession to be proud of. The restaurant business is more than a profession—it is a chosen lifestyle."

The creators of the Ella Brennan Savoir Faire Award stipulated that future winners should possess the same qualities of leadership and excellence as its namesake. So when the award was given in 1999, Ella Brennan had the honor of presenting it to Paul Prudhomme, once her executive chef and now a successful restaurateur, cookbook author, and businessman.

Ella also has a host of insights about the community and the hospitality industry. "America went through that awful period of convenience food after World War II," she recalls. But then came a renaissance. It began with such personages as James Beard, TV chef and cookbook author Julia Child, and California vintner Robert Mondavi. For Ella, they were the key influences who educated American palates and reshaped attitudes toward food. "This was the beginning of America becoming a great food country," she says, "and it's been going on ever since.

She pauses, then mentions another area where the Brennans have lent their support. "There has been an increased emphasis on cooking schools, too. We couldn't be more proud of the two CIAs [the Culinary Institute of America in Hyde Park, New York, and in St. Helena, California]. They are run with such professionalism."

For his part, Dick Brennan may be quiet, but his contribution to his industry has hardly gone unnoticed. In 1978, he was named to the Hall of Fame of the Louisiana Restaurant Association, which he had served as president in the 1960s. Dick and Ella's brother, Owen, also received the honor in 1978, and Ella was elected in 1987.

The Brennans are involved with national organizations as well. Dick was elected to the board of the National Restaurant Association in 1963, served until 1975, and then became an honorary director. Ella was a director from 1977 until 1983. Their nephew Ralph

■

Above right, Ella gives Paul Prudhomme a hug as she presents him with the Ella Brennan Savoir Faire Award. Below right, the Brennan women: Lauren Brennan Brower, Lally Brennan, Dottie Brennan-Bridgeman, Ella Brennan, Ti Martin, and Cindy Brennan.

"We've been raised to give back to the community as much as we can."—*Lally Brennan*

GREAT RESTAURANTS OF THE WORLD

Brennan, Lally's brother, succeeded Ella in 1984 and has been active on the board ever since.

The honors keep coming. In May 2000, the National Restaurant Association Educational Foundation inducted Ella into its College of Diplomates. According to the official statement, the Diplomates are "a select group of individuals who have distinctively enhanced the restaurant and hospitality industry by advocating education, training, and the sharing of knowledge."

By participating actively in civic organizations, the Brennans have made a lasting impact on the community. In the early 1960s, when Dick Brennan was president of the Louisiana Restaurant Association, he was instrumental in separating the city's tourist commission from the New Orleans Chamber of Commerce. That change enabled the commission, now called the New Orleans Metropolitan Convention and Visitors Bureau, to take a more active role in promoting the area not only nationwide but worldwide.

The next generation of Brennans is equally committed to supporting the hospitality industry and the community. "These kids all serve on boards, but they don't just put their names on the stationery," Ella says emphatically. "They get into it and they work." You can almost hear the subtext: They'd *better* work!

Not only do the younger members of the family take their civic responsibilities seriously but they often work together to carry them out. They take an active interest, for example, in the New Orleans Center for Creative Arts, which helps nurture local talent in vocal and instrumental music, composition, and dance. Among its graduates are

Commander's kitchen provides the ingredients for numerous worthy occasions in New Orleans.

trumpeter Wynton Marsalis, saxophonist Branford Marsalis, and singer Harry Connick, Jr. One year, Lally chaired a gala to raise money for the center, but the event was held at Storyville District, part of the Ralph Brennan Restaurant Group. Perhaps because of working together at the family's restaurants, the synergism comes naturally. "If Mr. B's Bistro is doing the event, we'll do another," says Lally. "That way, we can cover more."

Just as success comes in unexpected ways so, too, does recognition. The Brennans could hardly have expected their accomplishments to bring them to the attention of the state legislature. Yet that's what happened after they won the James Beard Foundation's award for Outstanding Restaurant in the United States. A resolution put forth by Rep. Mitch Landrieu, D-New Orleans, and passed unanimously by the Louisiana House of Representatives, states that "by being recognized as the standard of excellence for all fine-dining restaurants in the United States by industry experts," Commander's Palace and the Brennans have generated favorable publicity not just for themselves but for the city and the state. By simply being the best, they have done New Orleans and Louisiana proud.

Impressed by Commander's achievements, the
Louisiana House of Representatives passed a resolution
citing the restaurant's contribution to the area.

INDEX